Navigating Academic Leadership

Navigating Academic Leadership

How to Succeed
as a Department Chair
at a Research University

Sundar A. Christopher

The University of Alabama in Huntsville

Illustrations by Allison Jowers, Shaelyn Lozier, and Rachel Wyatt
Cover, book interior and ebook design by Booknook.biz

ISBN 979-8-218-35294-3

Dedication

This book is dedicated to several individuals who believed in me throughout my academic journey.

It's always scary to start listing individuals because I run the risk of forgetting someone important, but at the expense of not including someone, I would lose an opportunity to thank so many.

With that being said, along with a preemptive apology if I neglect to mention your name, here are the colleagues, friends, and family who have played significant roles in my journey and to whom I offer my deepest gratitude. To Dennis Musil, my first research adviser who believed in me and told me to hang on when the going was tough; to Ron Welch, who set the standards for research in my initial years; to every one of my graduate students—especially my PhD students—for pushing me to do good work; to my office mates, classmates, research collaborators, and program managers for their perpetual support; and to my friends and colleagues, Emanuel Waddell and John Maxon, who are shining examples of how to treat people well—a huge thank you.

Thank you to my kids—Grace, Samuel, and Abigail. Seeing you achieve things so much bigger than I ever could convinces me that this journey has been worth it. To my tireless champion, my wife Sheba, there are absolutely no words to describe what your love and support means to me. None of this would have been possible without you.

Very few places in this world would allow a first-generation immigrant like me to succeed with such humble beginnings. My sincerest appreciation to this great country of which I am proud to be a citizen: the United States of America!

Finally, I am eternally grateful for the Rock on which I stand because it was all miry clay before!

Sundar Christopher
Huntsville, Alabama

Contents

Preface

S ERVING AS DEPARTMENT CHAIR in an academic institution can be a fulfilling, exciting, and rewarding job. It could be an important stepping stone to future leadership positions. The department that you may end up leading could be small, perhaps with around 10 faculty members and 100 students, or large with multiple programs, dozens of faculty, and hundreds of students. Depending on the department's size, your job description may vary greatly. In small departments, your administrative team could be just you and a staff assistant. Larger departments could include assistant or associate department chairs supported by multiple staff assistants who manage budgets, coordinate fundraising, and direct outreach efforts. The combinations are endless.

If done well, the job of a department chair could be pivotal in laying the foundation for steady, successful operations. Done poorly, it can become a source of frustration to you and especially to others around you. Worse still, the department could begin a downward slide that could be detrimental in the long run. This book will help you prepare to be an effective department chair using case studies and practical advice on navigating this leadership position.

My personal career background includes many steps that ultimately led me to a department chair position. I finished my PhD in atmospheric science in the mid-1990s and started as an assistant professor at the University of Alabama in Huntsville (UAH). Through a linear career progression, I was promoted from assistant professor to associate professor with tenure and then quickly became a full professor. Soon I was also tapped to be the associate director of a major research center at UAH. On the heels of my professorship, I was appointed as department chair for a four-year term. Even though I was "promoted" to that position, I went through a rigorous interview process in which I had to write a position paper, give an hour-long presentation, and converse with students and other stakeholders. It was a useful experience because it allowed me to craft a vision plan that guided me as I stepped into the role.

I have always maintained a robust research program powered by significant external funding and numerous peer-reviewed papers. I've published well over 100 papers now—double that if you count conference papers. I continued to maintain an active research program even while I also completed a five-year term as dean of a college with about 100 faculties, seven departments, and 1500+ students. My interview process for deanship was even more rigorous than what I experienced as a department chair applicant, but I'll share more on that later. An academic career progression does not get any more linear than this! I decided to not continue climbing the administrative ladder (at least for a short time), and in 2019 I came back to the rank of professor to teach, mentor, serve, and lead a multimillion-dollar research program.

Both of my previous books, *Navigating Graduate School and Beyond* and *Navigating Tenure and Beyond: A Guide for Early Career Faculty*, have been practical guides filled with useful guidance. They present stories and situations one might typically encounter as a graduate student or young faculty member and offer advice for navigating various common issues. This book on academic leadership will be no exception.

I often get asked about how one can be ready to become a department chair and begin the journey as an administrative leader. In this book, I plan to not only cover topics on how to navigate the job of being a chair (after you are in the job) but also provide guidelines on figuring out if you are ready for the job, how to prepare for the application and interview processes, and how to transition to the actual job of a department chair. I will also provide some case studies that are typical in an administrative job which feature topics such as managing resource issues and handling confrontations with faculty and staff.

Not many universities have dedicated leadership programs that can help you figure out if you want to serve as an administrative leader and have the skill sets to do so. Most department chairs are simply "promoted" from professor to chair within their department. Some have the characteristics and skills that are needed to survive, thrive, and excel at the job. Others flounder because they have no frame of reference for working as a department chair, let alone being an effective one. In such a role, trial and error could prove costly. As scholars, we are used to reading and assimilating vast quantities of peer-reviewed papers, reports, and books, but when it comes to administrative and leadership matters, there is a lack of impetus to read and learn about these principles. I hope that as you begin this decision-making journey you not only read resources but also seek out mentors to help you with the process.

Finally, here are some caveats that are important for my readers to understand. There are numerous universities that are composed of colleges and departments. There is no one way to provide a general categorization for the various academic fields that are grouped in these colleges and departments because the nuances are immense. While teaching, research, creative achievements, and service are the cornerstones of American academic institutions, universities accomplish these endeavors in a variety of ways. While rankings and ratings exist in many formats, in my opinion, most of them fall short in capturing the very essence of why and how faculty operate to help university students succeed. Therefore, it is impossible to write a book and capture a specific department. This book provides many guidelines and practical tips for all department chairs, regardless of which department they are leading and serving. Based on what I have gleaned from my leadership roles and my discussions with department chairs around the country, it is clear that most department chairs face similar challenges.

In writing this book, I have aimed to be candid and upfront about topics, and I sincerely hope that you find it useful. Despite the challenges you may encounter, I also hope that you enjoy your role as department chair, because you have a rare opportunity to shape and mentor the next generation of faculty and students.

Author's Notes

1. **University organization.** Universities are organized into units in a myriad of ways. However, throughout this book, I have assumed that a college is a collection of departments. For example, a College of Engineering could include multiple departments such as Chemical Engineering, Industrial Engineering, Mechanical Engineering, etc., and each department is led by a department chair who reports to the Dean of the College. The dean, in turn, reports to the provost, who is usually the Executive Vice President for Academic Affairs. The provost manages multiple colleges, such as the College of Engineering, College of Business, College of Nursing, College of Arts, College of Sciences, etc. I have also assumed that, much like the Vice President for Academic Affairs (the provost) who reports to the President of the University, the Vice President of Research (VPR) also reports to the President. In some universities the VPR reports to the provost, and the titles may change slightly.

2. **Professorships.** In this book, I have assumed that a faculty member begins as an Assistant Professor in his or her first academic position. After a set number of years (typically six), the faculty member is considered for tenure and promotion to Associate Professor. Depending on the university, it takes a considerable period (maybe 10 years) to achieve the next faculty level, sometimes called Full Professor.

3. **Identities.** This book has numerous instances where I start a sentence like this: "As one department chair indicated…" or "As a faculty member said…" I hope my readers understand that this is not about any one university and especially not restricted to the university where I currently work. I continuously talk with department chairs and faculty around the country in various venues, and these examples come from my conversations with faculty, staff, department chairs,

and other administrators. More importantly, I have tried to provide case studies and examples that are merely hypothetical. Therefore, if you find yourself relating to a certain example or a situation, then this book is already a success!

Chapter 1.

Prerequisites for Being a Successful Department Chair

L ET ME ASSUME THAT you are a professor who has achieved tenure as an associate professor and has subsequently been promoted to full professor. If you want to move up to an administrative position, the most logical next step is to serve as department chair. (Later on, we will discuss the perils of stepping into a department chair role as an associate professor.)

Before you dive into the application process, start by seriously considering the question: *Are you ready to be a department chair?* If you are contemplating academic leadership, then serving as department chair is a great resumé-building step. However, *wanting to serve* as a department chair and *being ready* for the position are two separate things that are not always in alignment. Let's discuss some of the skill sets that you will need to build before going after that corner office and heftier paycheck!

I am assuming that you are already an expert in your field with strong credentials. But beyond that, you will need skills that will allow you to guide the department and mentor others. While you may possess excellent problem-solving skills in your area of research, serving as department chair will require something different—administrative problem-solving skills. The following job characteristics are typical for department head positions. How do your skill sets measure up in these categories?

- **Time management.** One of the most important prerequisites you will need is excellent time management skills. Whether you are teaching a few courses with a modest research program or managing a robust research program with a lighter teaching load, time management is critical to keep everything moving forward. Try asking folks around you to share their impression of *your* time management skills. Hopefully they will give you honest, useful feedback. If you are often late for appointments, struggle to balance work and life, or have difficulty providing timely replies to emails, the department chair job is not for you—at least not until you improve this skill set. As a department chair, there will be numerous demands on your time and attention. If you are already frustrated with time management in your current position, then you ought to rethink your department chair aspirations at this time. However, if you already practice solid time management methods, then you can mark this prerequisite as a yes!

- **People management.** This one can be complicated. If you are already managing a research team, then you should have acquired some expertise in how to run team meetings properly, set goals for the group, and motivate and empower team members to succeed. If you don't have any experience managing people now, then as a department chair you will be in for a shock and a steep learning curve. To be a successful department chair, you need to have an appetite for managing people, and you need to have a system in place now. If your current people management approach is more reactionary than methodical, then the chair job may not be for you yet. We will talk quite a bit about this aspect of being a department chair later in this book.

- **Deadline management.** Yes, there are even more things to manage! Currently as a professor and researcher you deal with numerous deadlines. If you travel to conferences, then you must fill out paperwork and manage all aspects of the travel process. If you write proposals, you must coordinate with the administration in your organization so you can submit on time. Your classes require meeting with students, maintaining office hours, and delivering timely feedback and grades. Preparing everything necessary to meet these deadlines can quickly become overwhelming. If you have a system in place that works to facilitate timeliness and limit stress, then you can check off this prerequisite box. Otherwise, you need to figure out better ways to manage your deadlines before seriously contemplating that department chair job. As chair, you will not only have to manage personal deadlines but also a whole host of departmental ones.

- **Work-life balance.** Nobody ever really feels like they maintain a perfect balance, but striving for a satisfying work-life balance *most* of the time should be the goal. If you struggle to remain holistically healthy, then the chair job will only heap on more stress. Without a commitment to doing what is necessary to achieve balance between your life inside and outside of the workplace, you don't stand a good chance of performing administrative duties well. One of the first things that department chairs sacrifice is their exercise regimen, which, in my opinion, is a dangerous thing to do. If you neglect to exercise regularly, there are bound to be detrimental effects that emerge quickly. Department chairs are also well known for not prioritizing scheduled vacations. A lack of down time will inevitably lead to unmanageable stress and ultimate burn out. The excuses are always the same: *I can't afford to take a vacation… There's too much to do! When I come back things will be piled up!* But no excuse is worth the risks that come with being overloaded and fatigued.

- **Sociability.** This category doesn't mean how many followers or connections you have on social media; instead, it encompasses the social intelligence and engagement you demonstrate in the workplace. You may consider yourself capable at the social aspects of your job if you already know how to network and talk to your peers about research. But as department chair, you will encounter a wider variety of social situations. You need to learn how to "get along" with your dean (who will be your boss), attend recruitment events, talk to potential donors, meet with concerned parents, console distressed students, and much more. These situations have nothing to do with research or network-

Striving for a sustainable work-life balance is a constant challenge for academic professionals.

ing, so you should be ready to adapt to any social circumstances. First impressions will never cease to be crucial, so don't forget that you will need to "dress the part." Gone are the days of wearing shorts and a t-shirt to work. Your favorite Hawaiian shirt should now be reserved for summer lawn parties or island vacations. Yes, on some days you will even have to wear a tie or, gasp, a formal suit! Plus, don't forget all those important dinners and events that you will be expected to attend at the dean's or president's house.

- **Confrontation management.** People groups and conflict go hand in hand, but a wise leader knows how to resolve and minimize disagreements when they arise. As a professor, all you generally have to think about is *your* teaching, research, and service portfolios. However, as department chair, you must always consider the collective good.

Here's what a department chair had to say. *"Sometimes faculty have a myopic view of the department. They usually want lighter teaching loads, a lot of resources (and some of that unrealistic), unending lab and office space, and administrative help at all times."*

Department chairs must manage their departments using limited resources that can change in scope and size each year. Therefore, being flexible in your approach is important. While it is not necessarily a prerequisite to already be a confident conflict manager before becoming a department chair, it is essential that you recognize the inevitability of conflict and the role you will have in addressing these situations. Trust me, your faculty will test you very quickly by confronting you with difficult requests and issues.

- **Process management.** Have you ever heard the phrase, *"The wheels of academia turn exceedingly slowly?"* It is absolutely true. Not only do the wheels turn slowly, but they are also mired in required procedures and lengthy processes. There are processes for complaints, travel, purchasing, course scheduling, and on and on. If you don't have an appetite for processes, you will starve! To stay on top of processes and the steps they involve, keep a copy of any relevant manuals or handbooks both at home and in your office. This will help you follow guidelines, identify questions, and avoid redoing work down the road. Also remember that just because something sounds efficient does not mean it will happen that way.

- **Work fragmentation.** As a professor with a busy schedule involving teaching, research, and service, you may think that you do not have enough hours in a day to keep everything running smoothly. Wait until you become a department chair! Your days become increasingly fragmented as you are pulled in many directions at once. Some enjoy the challenge of multi-tasking at an intense pace. Others are not ready for this. So, be forewarned that living with fragmented days is a reality in this position. As department chair, you become a piece of the puzzle in many decision-making processes both within and above your department. Between countless meetings and emails, it will often feel like you are not achieving any closure on just about anything. Patience is the key. You have to learn how to work in this new paradigm.

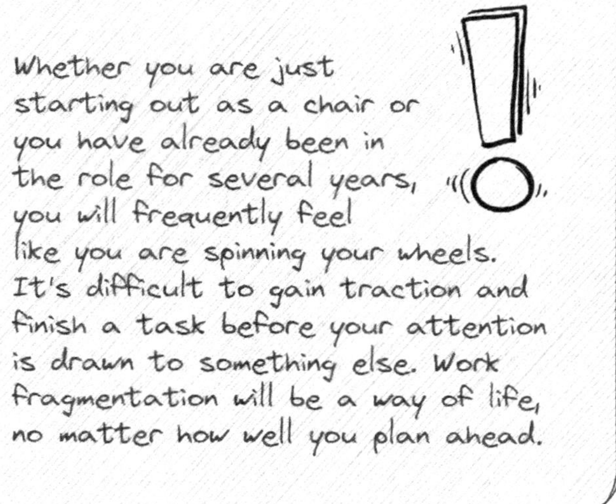

- **Mental stamina.** Trust me when I tell you—this job takes <u>a lot</u> of mental stamina. If you frequently find yourself complaining about the job of being a professor, the department chair job is definitely not for you. No one wants a department chair who constantly complains about job difficulty, troublesome faculty, and unrealistic administration expectations. Mental fortitude is necessary to maintain a positive attitude and adapt to job demands that may be in constant flux. If you doubt you can handle the stress expected at the department chair level, don't even apply for the position. As negative as it sounds, I hope it is construed as *"I wish someone had told me that earlier,"* or better yet, *"I am glad I read this sooner than later."* Understanding expected aspects of being an academic administrator before you pursue the job is imperative.

- **Championing initiatives.** This prerequisite especially applies to diversity, equity, and inclusivity (DEI) initiatives. As chair, you will be expected to recruit and mentor students and faculty with DEI frameworks in mind. Advocating for DEI should already be part of your core values. As chair, you will work with the office of DEI on your campus to be a champion for these causes. You must ensure that your faculty members understand the role that DEI plays in department affairs. If your university offers DEI training, take advantage of this service, and encourage all your department members to do so as well. Going through the same training will ensure that your whole department is aware of how DEI impacts everyone in the workplace. If no training opportunities are available, your university's human resources department may be able to lead a relevant seminar.

- **Emotional intelligence.** I conversed with one department chair who discussed the importance of emotional intelligence in department chairs. In the modern-day workplace, the ability to understand and manage emotions effectively is important. Self-awareness and empathy will allow department chairs to navigate interpersonal issues and build trust more effectively within a department.

Let me wrap this section up for now by saying that if you already know that you are not great at managing time, people, deadlines, and confrontation, then the timing is probably not right for a transition to academic leadership. These are some necessary prerequisites for the job, and if you do end up with the chair job, these weaknesses will frustrate you and others around you.

The You Factor—Your physical, mental, and emotional well-being

Recently I had a long conversation with a department chair who was ready to quit his job as chair and return to the rank of professor. This is the proverbial "walking on the ledge scenario," where the only solution in the chair's mind was to quit. My job was to coax the chair off the ledge into a safe space so perspective would prevail, and he might continue as chair. The conversation mostly involved me listening while he shared his frustrations. Here is part of our conversation:

Chair: *Do you have a minute, and can I shut the door?*
Me: *Please come in and have a seat.*
Chair: *I hope this will not take long, but I hope you can give me some advice.*
Me: *Of course.*
Chair: *I am totally stressed out. I've been chair for about four years now, and lately it has been taking a toll on me. I have not been able to exercise for a long time now, and recently my doctor has put me on hypertension (blood pressure) medication. To make matters worse, I don't even find the time to eat a proper meal during the day, and I go home exhausted! I recently had to start on cholesterol medication as well. Even though I try to take short breaks or vacations, I end up working during those times. I am seriously thinking about quitting my job as chair and returning to being a professor again.*
Me: *Wow, it sounds like you have an awful lot to manage right now. Tell me a bit more about what in particular is causing you stress at work.*
Chair: *Just about everything is getting to me these days. Faculty are constantly complaining about one thing or another. Recently, a faculty member was in my office yelling about office space and access for one of his students to a laboratory. Another faculty member always wants more resources and drains my time because she is constantly in my*

office wanting to talk about the same thing over and over. Another faculty member wants more pay, and the dean wants more and more reports and information all the time. I don't have any help running the department. It is only me and my administrative assistant. I really could use an associate chair to handle some of this job, so I don't completely burn out.

Department chairs are often bombarded by everyone's requests, opinions, and complaints.

I am going to pause this dialog to offer some perspective. Before you think that all department chairs experience such issues, I want to assure you that this is not the case. In this situation, it appears that this chair has been trying to manage a lot in his leadership role. From the chair's perspective, the job-related matters have negatively affected his physical, mental, and emotional health. Clearly, he needs support in figuring out how to regain satisfaction in both his job and life. This is why academic coaching and mentoring can play important roles in identifying issues and facilitating change. Let's discuss some basics of how to take care of yourself so you can be of help to others.

1. The first thing to realize, and probably something you should repeat to yourself many times, is that your career follows a *long arc*. What do I mean by that? Remember that your career will likely span multiple decades, and serving as an administrator is only a comparatively small portion of that career. Therefore, burning yourself out over the short term will only damage your career in the long term. It's just not worth it.

2. The second thing to remember is that there is no such thing as a perfect organization or a perfect group of people that you are going to manage or lead. Faculty, staff, students, and various stakeholders all have their own perspectives, which will always generate friction, miscommunication, and controversies. You need to realize that when leading people, some amount of stress is unavoidable, so managing that stress should be a priority.

3. Finally, realizing that we work within non-optimal systems is important. Resources may be limited, processes may be slow and frustrating, and mistakes will be made. It is up to you to navigate and manage these issues. Thinking about possible bottlenecks and potential problems ahead of time could help you prevent some complications before they even occur. However, if you spend too much time predicting and troubleshooting problems, you will tend to micromanage and wear yourself out. Therefore, striking a balance is critical.

An important part of the You Factor is recognizing that maintaining your personal health is vital. This next section is purposefully written in a coaching format to offer tips for addressing some common issues that arise when working in a demanding managerial role.

Managing your physical health. Administrators either realize that this needs to be at the very top of their list, or they simply don't. Managing your calendar well to schedule time for physical exercise ought to be a high priority because research has shown that it boosts mood, improves cognitive function, and lowers a myriad of health risk factors. Let's consider a few different health management approaches.

1. **"Highest Priority" Chair.** This type of department chair consistently maintains a healthy physical lifestyle. She never misses a workout, scheduling it either first thing in the morning or at the end of her workday. She is also conscious about what she eats and drinks throughout the day. Her lifestyle naturally encourages others around her, including her faculty, to take care of their physical bodies as well. She understands that even during stressful times of the academic year when multiple deadlines are looming, her exercise regimen should not be neglected. Even when she occasionally has to miss a workout session due to travel or sickness, she makes sure that she quickly gets back into her routine. The "highest priority" mentality provides her many benefits despite being sometimes difficult to maintain.

   Many academic leaders work out regularly, setting aside time before or after work for physical activity. I know an administrator who plays racquetball for about an hour three days a week starting at 6:45 AM. Several other managers I know look forward to "hitting the gym" at the end of each workday. A "highest priority" active chair told me, "*I have no idea how people deal with stressful days if they have not worked out earlier in the day and put the correct type of food in their bodies. I can tackle my problems a lot better with clarity of mind when I make work out priority.*" Between meetings and daily demands, it can be nearly impossible to squeeze in exercise during the middle of the day. However, I know a department chair who swims five days a week for 30 to 45 minutes during her lunch hour. Regardless of scheduling demands, it's possible to create a sustainable and enjoyable exercise plan.

   Eating out at restaurants several times a month is often part of the job as well, so "highest priority" chairs are careful to choose healthier meal options. Bringing lunches from home also helps limit impulses to rely on vending machine snacks and fast food for sustenance. Now, before you start thinking that you must run marathons, become a tennis sensation, or earn your black belt in martial arts, I want to emphasize that working out does not have to be complex. It should always be something that you enjoy. Even something as simple as walking is a beneficial exercise option. Also, consider joining a group, club, or class that will hold you accountable. Your university probably has some convenient fitness programs and facilities on site to enable you to make your health the "highest priority."

2. **"Lowest Priority" Chair.** In her daily schedule, working out is the "last priority" item for this chair. Despite reading articles that explain how exercise is linked to better stress management, she finds herself unable to make her health a priority. Her calendar is always full of work-related items, and even if she does manage to schedule physical activity, she allows that plan to get wiped out by any other demand. A "lowest priority" chair's perspective on health management often sounds something like, "*How am I supposed to put together a workout schedule if there are so many problems and issues to deal with daily? As chair, all I have is an administrative assistant for support, and with no other help I am left to tackle all the problems that keep cropping up. Even when I do my best to put a workout session on my calendar, another problem comes my way, and I sacrifice my workout time for the good of the department.*" I am sure some of you reading this can relate to these situations.

I realize that there will always be "fires that need to be put out": another phone call to take, another meeting to attend, or another document to draft. The list of things that require your attention will always be long, but you have to—absolutely have to—realize that unless you are healthy physically, you will have a lot of difficulty managing the stress associated with this position. Think of exercising regularly as putting on your oxygen mask first so you can help others around you. Prioritizing your personal health is, in essence, also prioritizing the health of your entire department. This is why you should learn to manage your calendar diligently and create an expectation that your work out time cannot be compromised.

3. **"Start and Stop" Chair.** This type of chair understands the value of taking care of his physical health and has good intentions to make it a priority. While working out typically lands in the "top ten" items on his priority list, he struggles to maintain consistency. This chair tends to follow a pattern in which he schedules time to work out and follows through initially, but then a variety of factors begin to erode his commitment. Eventually he realizes that he hasn't exercised in days or weeks. Frustrated by the way he feels, he begins the cycle all over again.

Here's what one "stop and start" chair had to say. *"I had an excellent mentor who emphasized the value of physical exercise. He talked about how important exercise was to an administrator and the benefits he experienced—better sleep, increased energy and the ability to manage stress well. I followed through with this advice in the beginning and I started well, getting up early to exercise before I headed to work. But then things at work took priority, and I would stop. My stress levels would mount, and my sleep patterns would be disrupted. I would start back again, and every time I restarted my work out regime it was that much harder to get back into it. Then I would repeat the pattern for a while—starting and stopping—and I eventually gave up working out."*

While some exercise is certainly better than none at all, an emotional toll can be inflicted by repeatedly struggling to establish a routine. Next, let's examine your holistic health by considering how to prioritize your mental health along with your physical well-being.

Managing your mental health. Every department chair must take this seriously because you need to be healthy emotionally and mentally to effectively lead a group of people. Constant stress not only complicates physical health but also slowly wears down your cognitive function and your ability to control your emotions.

Making your mental health a priority is critical, because if you are not healthy, then the negative effects could spill over to the rest of the department. Seek support and advice when needed, and practice deliberate stress management measures on a regular basis. For some this could be exercise, while others may find meditation and other types of relaxation techniques useful. Probably the hardest thing to do is to say "no" to things, but it helps set appropriate boundaries in your professional life. Some of the most valuable advice that I believe I can offer you in this book is this: manage your time (and calendar) effectively. It goes a long way in reducing stress.

Being aware of your mental health status is the first step to managing it well. Most universities offer programs and even opportunities to meet with therapists to help you better understand and monitor your mental health. Be sure to review your health insurance plan so you are aware of all the benefits available before you may need them. Some telltale signs often indicate that you are experiencing emotional wear and tear:

1. **Irritability.** If you are generally an even-keeled person (you almost *need* to have this quality to be a department chair!) and find yourself getting irritated about even the smallest things, then it's time to assess your stress levels. As an administrator, it's wise to conduct periodic "irritability gut checks" by thinking about the tone and language you are using with other administrators, faculty, staff, and students. Remember that you have a broad set of constituents that you are serving. Your days will often be filled with addressing the needs of others, which can sometimes be frustrating. The first hour of your day could involve a tedious discussion with a disgruntled faculty member while your administrative assistant is knocking on your door because the Dean needs to speak with you. Just as all that simmers down, a student problem may suddenly require your intervention while you receive emails about your overdue travel authorization forms. Whew! Each situation needs careful attention and a balanced outlook. If you are irritable and end up "snapping" at anyone, then it's time to find a way to reduce your stress by going for a short walk, listening to some music, or simply closing your office door for a short time.

2. **Considering quitting.** If you constantly think about quitting your job because of the various pressures you experience and you begin to vocalize this at home and at work, then it's time to assess your mental health. I realize that there are times when most people are discon-

tented with their work situations. However, if you find thoughts of quitting to be foremost on your mind during most of your days, and if it persists for long periods of time, then this is a strong sign that your mental health is deteriorating and needs to be addressed.

Elevated stress levels can cause you to fixate on the idea of quitting your job.

3. **Feeling depressed.** If you have feelings of depression that are persistent and beyond the normal wear and tear of academic administration, it may be time to seriously consider seeing a professional who can provide you with support and tools to address this issue. Discounting mental health and ignoring signs of depression will only make matters worse.

4. **Negative outlook and cynicism.** If you begin to feel like you're seeing everything through a negative filter with an added layer of cynicism, this also could be a sign of emotional burnout. Even worse, your negativity and cynicism could spread through your department from fac-

ulty to students and beyond. One of the first places to watch out for such negativity is how you interact with your administrative assistant. A constant pessimistic attitude can damage your relationship with this person that you will rely on for considerable support and may cause him or her to become less satisfied with their job as well.

5. **Feeling detached and unmotivated.** At times it may seem that as department chair you are battling the whole world, or you versus the rest of the university. When things are not going well, that feeling is normal, but if it becomes pervasive on a day-in, day-out basis, then you ought to reassess your mental and emotional health. Feelings of detachment and motivation can quickly lead to a lack of productivity and general negativity. Worse still, you may begin to do the absolute minimum at work, limit your office hours, and dread coming into work at all. These could all be signs of burnout. A while ago when I asked a department chair how she was doing, she responded this way: "*Things are too hectic at work, and I feel totally burned out. I cannot seem to peel away from work to take a break and recharge my batteries. Lately, I have been contemplating quitting, and I don't even want to do the basic stuff as chair anymore, let alone the important ones. I guess I am in withdrawal mode already. Plus, to make matters worse, I don't want to interact with anyone, and I feel like I am isolating myself. I've never been one to shirk responsibilities, but I am already there.*" This is indeed a serious case of emotional and mental exhaustion.

Managing your mental and emotional health is extremely important for you and others around you. If you recognize these symptoms and are not willing to put together a plan to mitigate these issues, this situation will likely deteriorate further. For some, simply taking a complete break for a short time—whether a few days or a couple of weeks—could allow enough time to mentally "reset" and return to work with a new perspective and increased motivation. For others, it may require a longer break, and unfortunately for others, it may mean having to leave the job entirely because the stress factors in the job are too many. However, the most important thing to realize is that your health is more important than the job itself. Walking away from a situation like this should not be construed as a failure but as a victory in self-awareness and the emphasis you place on your health.

Why do you want to be a department chair?

This is a serious question that you need to answer before you embark on the journey of applying for the department chair position or becoming one. There is really no right or wrong answer to this question, but recognizing your own, true answer may require some soul searching. Here are some authentic answers to this question that I have heard:

- **Nobody else wants the job.** If you think this response is a bit extreme, you are in for a surprise. In many departments where faculty are busy with teaching and research or have no appetite for administrative roles, this is indeed the case. No one wants the job because they're afraid of the paperwork that it entails and having to march to someone else's drum. Faculty can shy away from the job for a variety of reasons, so you may consider taking on the challenge. Plus, research-active faculty are often not ready to give up their research productivity to become administrators.

- **I want the pay raise.** This is true in most cases. As a faculty member on a nine-month academic appointment, you must acquire funding for the remaining three months through grants and contracts. If your probabilities to win proposals are declining, you may be tempted to become a department chair because it pays a 12-month salary. You should be careful, though, because your university could elect to pay your salary in a variety of ways. Depending on the complexity of the payment method, you may need to do some calculations and weigh the pros and cons. Below are some possible ways that your salary could be structured.

Method 1: Take your 9-month salary (base salary), and multiply by 1.33 to determine your 12-month salary. So, if your 9-month salary was

$100,000, then your 12-month salary will be $133,000. Remember, when you are no longer department chair, you will go back to your 9-month salary.

Method 2: Same as Method 1, but with an added stipend. In this case, your 12-month salary could be $133,000 plus a stipend (let's use $12,000 as an example). Your annual salary would be $145,000. When you go back to being a 9-month faculty member, the 33% multiplicative factor and stipend would be gone.

In both methods described above, you make a better salary during your four years as chair, but your base salary structure does not change. Also, to fully understand these methods, you need to have a clear understanding of how pay raises are distributed. Will there be a pay raise for the stipend or not? To which portion of the pay is the raise calculated?

Method 3: In this method, your base salary is increased, and the 1.33 multiplicative factor is applied to your new base pay. You may even receive a stipend on top of this amount. This is probably the best package from your vantage point. When you go back to the 9-month faculty position, your base salary will be higher than before. You could argue that you need an adjustment to your base; after all, your research productivity is going to decrease while you are a department chair. But it all depends upon how well you can negotiate, how desperately your department needs you as chair, and what the governing policies dictate. If you are not comfortable with the pay structure, then it's best to make an informed decision in the beginning rather than setting yourself up for disappointment.

- **The alternative is horrifying.** Ahh!! The horror option. While your department was possibly humming along with an effective department chair, she may have decided to retire or move to another university. Your dean then told the department that the next chair must be one of the current faculty members. No one was interested except that totally disorganized faculty member (with zero leadership or communication skills) who wants the job just for the money. As one of the senior faculty members, you even try to "recruit" another faculty member to step up and be chair, but no one is interested. Caught between a rock and a hard place, you decide to accept the role yourself. Some of you might have been reading this section with a wry smile and thinking—yep, that's me!

- **This is my stepping stone to future administrative positions.** Let's say that you are the type of person who has a career plan mapped out, and at the end of that road, you plan to be the vice president or president of a university. Therefore, the department chair position is the first step in that path. We need more faculty who have this kind of ambition. Some consider working through the administrative chain of command very similar to the process of working through tenure and promotion to professor. You were likely hired just after you finished your PhD, or you moved from another organization. Either way, you will spend your time working through teaching, research, and being engaged as a colleague and a citizen of your department within a broader university context.

  If you desire and decide to become a department chair, this is usually the logical next step, unless there are other leadership opportunities such as being an assistant/associate chair in your department or an assistant/associate dean in your college. Be careful about leaping directly into a dean position, though. It is important to serve a full term as a department chair—usually 4 or 5 years—before you think about the next level as a dean. It may be tempting to skip deanship completely and apply for a vice president position (provost or VP of research), but this is usually not a good idea. Working through the appropriate levels hones your skill to be an effective leader. If you skip being a department chair and go directly to a dean position, you really cannot understand the nuances of a department budget and how to work with faculty. Similarly, if you go straight from being a department chair to a VP position and skip the dean level, you will miss learning critical lessons about leadership and communication as a dean. Unless you are an unusually skilled administrator, skipping any administrative position level will produce knowledge gaps that will show in your decision-making processes. The department chairs that you lead in your college will quickly figure out that you have never served as chair, if some of the decisions that you make are based solely on university goals and objectives, not based on a thorough understanding of the department.

A colleague of mine who served as a university dean shared the following experience.

"I was surprised when they appointed the provost because she had never been a department chair or a dean, for that matter. She was an associate provost of some sort at another university and had no responsibilities as a 'line manager'. She seemed eager to engage the deans, but very quickly we found out as deans that she was out of her depth. She had difficulty negotiating the parameters of a college budget and did not really understand faculty course loads. Worse still, she had no idea how the research mission of the university fit within the teaching (academic) part of the university. She worked tirelessly but was inefficient. She did not know how to manage and ended up micro-managing everything. I had a very difficult time as dean because she was not interested in the 30,000 ft. view of the academic enterprise and mostly paid attention to the 'small stuff.'"

He went on to say that, while she seemed eager to work hard as provost, her lack of experience at the chair and dean levels clearly showed in her day-to-day decision-making capabilities. While I am sure there are examples of administrators who have successfully skipped a level or two, it is rarely the case. Learning the job at every level is crucial to become an effective administrator.

Department chairs sometimes want to serve as deans to make a difference and exercise their leadership skills at the next level, and some simply wish to revert to a professor position after having served one term as chair. Here is what a department chair who did not want to move the next level of administration had to say: *"I realized that leading a department had challenges, and I was ready for it, but the sheer number of faculty who seem to be squabbling about trivial matters and filing grievances against one another left me exhausted.*" While this may be an extreme case of faculty turmoil, as chair, you must realize that managing a department does not just involve setting a vision and executing it. People have to be managed, motivated, and empowered, and sometimes disciplinary actions are necessary.

- **I like to manage units within organizations.** Leading and managing groups within organizations is an interest or a particular skill set that you possess. You have an eye for streamlining processes, and you are ready to eliminate inefficiencies. Leading from the front is something that you genuinely enjoy. Of course, the department chair job is something that you should try if you have these types of skill sets! I am sure that you have noticed that not everyone can stay organized. Upper management (administrators and senior personnel) in organizations are always looking for good leadership material. The first thing that they look at is not just your success in academia but how well you manage multiple tasks and how you present yourself before stakeholders.

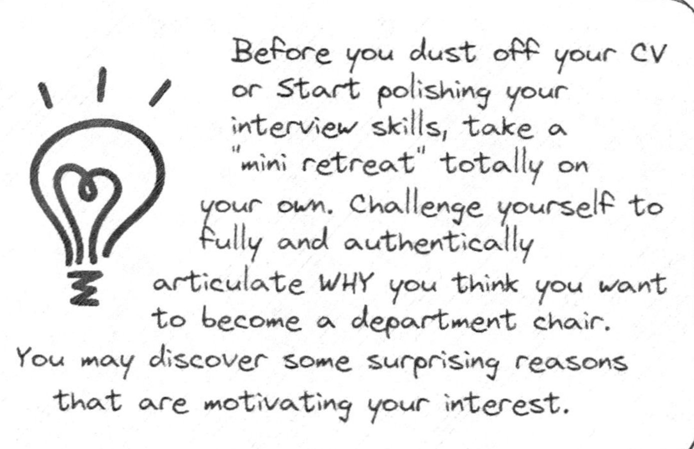

- **I need an outlet for my leadership skills.** You have innate leadership skills that need an outlet, and you are always looking for opportunities to lead. Serving as department chair may be a natural fit with your skillset. Sometimes you may not be the next in line for the department chair job at your university, and it can be difficult to wait for a long period of time before you get your opportunity. You may eventually have to consider leaving the university to seek other leadership possibilities. Other universities may actually recruit you to serve as a department chair. Being prepared to serve as chair is probably the best way to position yourself for success. Most colleges are looking for a competent leader with excellent credentials, but more importantly, they seek someone who works well with people and who has a forward-thinking vision for the department.

- **I want to save a flailing department.** You have been a faculty member for several years, and due to lack of leadership (or other reasons) you've watched the department languish. Because you care about your colleagues and the university, you want to take on the challenge of righting the ship, so to speak. This is a noble mentality, but it can be dangerous to view yourself as a necessary "savior." There's nothing wrong in wanting to save a floundering department, and often a champion is needed to accomplish this job. However, it is important to realize that not everyone is good at cleaning up problems.

- **I'm ready to "do my part".** Most of the time a department chair is selected from within the existing faculty because the university feels that the person in this administrative position should be familiar with the faculty, staff, and students. It is also quite possible that there are one or more good internal candidates for the job with the appropriate credentials and mindset. Some departments even have an unwritten understanding that if you have been in the department for a while, it will eventually be your turn to serve as chair for a few years and then step down from the position for the next faculty member to take her place. This system generally works if there is enough faculty who are willing to rotate into the chair position for a few years and slide back into their faculty positions. It also works well because everyone clearly understands that the faculty members are doing this as a service to the department. Operating like this means that there are usually minimal problems between the chair and the faculty; after all, it may be your turn next. However, this system also assumes that the faculty member rotating into the position has the appetite and the skill sets for the position and that they will do the job diligently.

- **The department needs an outsider (like me).** When the department or university looks for a person outside of the department to install as chair, there could be various agendas in mind. For example, the department may feel that this is an opportunity to attract a high-profile candidate with excellent research credentials. Sometimes these individuals can come from the "industry." Business schools may be especially interested in recruiting someone from a Fortune 500 company to serve as a department chair. These types of candidates may be excellent businesspeople and skilled negotiators, but they may only have an undergraduate or master's degree (rather than the expected PhD).

  There may be a plan for this person to come and raise funds for the department and develop strong ties to the business community. While this often happens at the dean and upper administrative levels, depending upon the university, this is also possible at the chair level. Everyone in the department needs to discuss their views concerning what they think the priorities of the next department chair should be before the selection process starts so that there is a clear understanding of the role of the next chair. It is important to realize that this person may not be a "scholar" in the sense that the department defines this term, but the new chair will have other skills that may be applied to achieve success. Since this person could have less experience in academic matters, an associate chair may be needed to handle the day-to-day affairs of the department while the chair establishes connections to the community and raises funds for the department and university. Coming from another sector (e.g., industry) to lead the department has several advantages and disadvantages, and it is up to the faculty to identify and address as many foreseeable issues as possible before hiring. After all, if the new chair raises a lot of funds, enrollment can increase, and more funds may be available for new facilities, upgraded equipment, additional faculty lines, etc.—all of which will be beneficial to the department.

- **I needed a change.** I am tired of writing papers and proposals and teaching courses, and I want to try my hand at administration. While this statement seems a bit drastic, some professors do feel this way. After a couple of decades of teaching and research, a faculty member can get weary of the routine and want to try something different— academic administration. While trying something new may bring rejuvenation, it is important to make sure that you have the credentials, appetite, skill sets, and mindset to be a department chair. You will quickly realize that you have exchanged the things that you can mostly control (e.g., research, writing, and presenting) for things that you have very little control over, such as operating budgets and college and university policies.

  Also, it is important to be mindful of the career stage in which you are wanting to make a change. If things do not work out as department chair, then you have only a few options left: return to professorship or try looking for another administrative job. Depending upon where you are in your career, you could even consider retirement! Sometimes even university presidents return to their original department to become faculty again, so a "homecoming" to teaching and research is not uncommon. Now, if you abandon your research completely as a department chair, it will be very challenging to jump start your research career again because research moves much too quickly in most disciplines. Therefore, the "I need the change" paradigm requires careful consideration.

- **I want to leave town due to a personal situation** and move to another place to become department chair at a different university. I have seen this happen in a few situations when the current job as chair or a professor just does not pan out due to a family or personal situation. Life happens! When deciding to move, timing is critical, and sometimes there is little time for planning. Applying for a job at another university may not be a problem, but it is important to remember that the process will involve lengthy interviews and decision-making processes that can require months to finalize.

- **The current chair of my department is incompetent.** Admit it. Some of you smiled at this section heading. I once heard a faculty member say, *"My department chair is so incompetent, he can't tie his shoelaces straight."* As dramatic as this sentiment was, it is sometimes true that a change in leadership is needed at the department level because the current chair either can't or won't fulfill their duties. It's time for a change! As a professor, your view of how a department chair performs her duty may be very different from reality. Unless you actually sit at the desk of a department chair and do the job, it is almost possible to know what is required of a chair and how to approach and accomplish tasks.

Be careful of judging someone in a leadership position until you have tried shouldering their responsibilities yourself.

Various factors should be assessed when wanting to step into the role of department chair, especially if the current chair has performed inadequately. This means that there will be a lot of "mopping up" to do when you become chair. Processes may be weak or nonexistent, morale may be low, and standards may have deteriorated. To make matters worse, no one in the college or the university may take the department seriously because of the previous chair's actions or lack thereof. In a situation like this, things can only go up because the department has already hit rock bottom in many aspects. While this may be seen as a good opportunity for you to move the department in a positive direction, be warned that the work ahead will be substantial. Just about everything needs to be evaluated, and many action plans must be drafted. If this "clean up" duty doesn't seem like something you would like to manage, then do not take on the role. However, mending the department is something that needs to be done, and the collective good of all people involved is important. As a colleague of mine put it, "*If you are not willing to step up and take care of the department, then quit complaining.*" Point well taken.

- **I am still an associate professor, but I feel ready to step into a leadership position.** This can be a complicated situation depending on the circumstances in your department and at your university. Sometimes there are no other options. You may be in a department that has a few assistant and a few associate professors, and the only (full) professor who served as department chair abruptly left for some legitimate reason. You may be the only option to shepherd the department for a few years. In general, let me repeat, in general, it is not a good idea for an associate professor to lead a department, especially if there are full professors in the department. However good you may be (or think you may be) at leading a department, you have not yet maximized your credentials in your department. In most departments, the climb from associate to full professor may be steep because you have to demonstrate that you are a leading authority in your area of expertise. As an associate professor, you are yet to cross that threshold. Therefore, regardless of your management skills, it will be difficult for your faculty to accept your leadership without harboring some doubt (regardless of what they might say directly to you or each other). If possible, it is better to wait until you are promoted to full professor before pondering leadership roles.

Serving as interim department chair

At some point you may have the opportunity to don the mantle of an "unofficial" department chair by serving in an interim role while the university goes through a formal search process. By definition, interim means "in the meantime." Interim positions can take on many forms, and you should be fully aware of the details and potential consequences of stepping into this type of role. Usually, the current department chair leaves because he found another job, felt "done" with being chair, or was promoted to the next level. Maybe there is not enough time to initiate a search process for a department chair, or perhaps the current chair resigns in the middle of the academic year. Whatever the reason may be, the dean may not be ready to select the next department chair for a full term. The dean and department faculty agree that someone within the department should serve as interim chair until they initiate a formal search for a more permanent chair.

It is important to have a clear understanding of how long the interim position is intended to last. Typically, a dean will decide that an interim chair will remain in place for about one year or until a proper candidate search can be conducted. The dean may be true to her word and stick to this timeline, but sometimes the position will be extended for two or more years because a search could not be completed or negotiations with a candidate failed.

When considering an interim chair position, you should ask yourself two questions. Why do I want to serve as interim chair? And do I want the job as a department chair without the interim title someday, or am I just doing this until a chair can be selected? If you feel that you have satisfying answers to these questions, you should also consider the following potential outcomes of serving as an interim chair.

1. **You are appointed later as department chair.** The lease-to-own option! In this case, everyone generally understands that you will serve

as department chair for an appropriate amount of time until certain procedures can be completed, and then you will be appointed as full department chair. The process usually involves open nominations for candidates, and if you are the only one nominated, then the path to becoming full chair will be smooth (typically). However, if one of your faculty colleagues decides to throw her name into the hat, then a more complicated process follows that will include interviews and faculty voting.

2. **You serve only for a short period of time.** If you find yourself in this position, there is still a job to do as interim chair. Maybe you communicate clearly that you do not want to be a department chair after the interim position is complete, or perhaps you just want to try the position for a year to gain some insight and experience. Whatever the case may be, everyone around you knows that you are in this interim position to help steward the department for a short time until a new chair can be found. The dean will probably task you to lead efforts to recruit the next department chair, which could turn into a national search.

   It is important to remember that even though you have an "interim" title, the duties of being a chair must still be handled—from course assignments to faculty negotiations, managing budgets to dealing with student-related matters. The number of meetings will increase because you will be required to meet with the dean and other administrators around campus regarding department-related matters. Meanwhile, you will still need to maintain your job as a professor—teaching and conducting research. After all, when the job of an interim chair is over, you will return to your regular role.

   While it goes without saying that the job of an interim chair is to hold the position until a permanent chair can be selected, I have known some interim chairs to initiate strategic plans, realign budgets, and effectively do the job of a permanent chair. This approach can be treacherous, because when the new chair arrives, she may decide to institute new measures that could cause confusion and lead to undoing much of the work previously done. It is customary that your dean recognizes the additional responsibilities of serving as interim chair and compensates you in the form of a stipend on top of your regular salary. If no stipend is mentioned, then take the initiative to ask, even if it makes you feel "uncomfortable," because it's better to be informed as you step into the role and avoid potential disappointment.

3. **You are reappointed to be interim chair for another year, and another year...** You get the picture, right? You agreed to serve for one year as interim chair because the department needed a steady hand at the helm. Everyone was happy, and you took on additional responsibilities because you are interested in the collective good of the department. You led the search for the next department chair while continuing to do all your other work as a professor. A reasonably good pool of candidates was collected and interviewed, and you presented a short list of three candidates to the dean. Despite your diligent efforts to recruit your replacement, the stars just don't align. Your first choice accepts a job elsewhere, the second candidate renegotiates with her current university and withdraws her application, and negotiations simply break down with the third candidate because he wants more salary and resources than your college can afford. The process took so long that there was no time to revisit the applicant pool and restart the process to find the next chair before the next academic year begins.

As interim chair, you are now stuck. Your faculty and dean are looking to you to continue your interim chair role, and who knows, at this point they may decide to offer you the opportunity to become full chair. Perhaps you've impressed them so far with your efforts, and it is nearly impossible to recruit a new chair in the middle of the academic year anyway. If you're asked to extend your stay in the role of interim chair, though, it's time for you to make a judgment call. You know the pressures and intensity that come with the job of interim chair because you have already done it for a year, and you also know how protracted and demanding the recruitment process can be. You're also aware of the challenges in maintaining your research and teaching portfolios while being interim chair.

You have very few choices, but it is essential that you determine the correct one for your situation. If you take on this role for another year, you should realize that there could be another failed search at the end of that year, and then you will have to go through this decision process all over again. The other option is to tell your faculty and the dean that it is someone else's turn to be interim chair. This second option is better if you have no intention of becoming a chair soon and if your work as a professor has suffered during your time as interim chair. However, most interim chairs are unable to make a clear-cut decision for various reasons—a sense of responsibility, the financial incentive of a stipend, or simply the excitement of being connected to higher administrative levels at the university. The reasons for staying on as interim department chair need to be genuine and carefully considered, otherwise there will be negative implications for the department and university.

Some serious questions

I said at the beginning (and still maintain) that the department chair job can be rewarding, fulfilling, and exciting. But at the same time, you need to seriously think about how becoming chair *will* change not only your life, but also the lives of others in your personal and professional circles. Often administrators think that a job is exclusively about their aptitude and performance. However, as a leader of your unit, you will affect and influence many people around you. Doing your job well while balancing all other facets of your life will stimulate growth in yourself and the people who are connected to you. Doing your job poorly will surely produce negative consequences. Taking the time to pose and answer some serious questions about yourself is not just recommended but truly necessary before accepting a department chair position.

- **Do you possess the ideal credentials?** Having a PhD and holding the title of professor does not necessarily mean that you have the best credentials for being a department chair. Let's say you work in a department where the emphasis is on a successful graduate program rather than significant dedication to undergraduate education. This probably means that the faculty are focused on fostering research productivity and reputation through top-notch peer-reviewed publications, invited presentations, grant acquisition, and perhaps book authorship. Let's also assume that while faculty teach graduate students, the job of teaching undergraduates is left to either lecturers or part-time instructors. If your credentials fit how success is measured in this type of department, then you have nothing to worry about. However, if your credentials might be considered weak or at least a mismatch with departmental priorities, then you should rethink your next steps.

  Remember that, while in most departments, faculty are evaluated on their teaching, research, and service portfolios, in a graduate education and research-focused department, research accomplishments are weighted more heavily. This means that faculty are expected to write proposals to funding agencies and secure research funding because they are teaching fewer classes and handling a lighter service load. The expectations in a research-focused department are usually completely different from a teaching-focused department. National and international reputations are highly valued in such departments, and the quality and quantity of peer-reviewed publications are also critical. Later, we will discuss how these factors are often used in faculty evaluation. Therefore, if your peer-reviewed publications and proposals won are not up to par with the expectations of such a department, your credentials will not be recognized as a sufficient match for the department.

Depending upon the department that you currently work in or one that you may end up in later as chair, it may take a long time to earn trust as a department chair. If you have inadequate credentials, then you have an uphill climb to begin with, and you may have to invest considerable effort to gain the confidence of your faculty. This is why you need to be aware of how success is measured in your department and make sure that your credentials match well.

Also, being promoted to department chair without incident or argument does not mean that the faculty are going to be fully on board with every action you take as department chair. Dynamics are subject to change, even among the same faculty who wanted you to become the department chair and pledged their assistance in managing departmental matters. Even your most vociferous supporters can scurry back to their quiet lives as professors, leaving you to supervise all aspects of the department with little or no faculty support.

- **Are you willing to reduce your research productivity?** If you have a vibrant research program with adequate research funding to support a team of graduate students, postdocs, and scientists, then you undoubtedly worked hard to get to this point. You have written numerous proposals and peer-reviewed papers, and you travel (a lot) as you attend and present at numerous conferences. This is what success looks like. The university applauds your research productivity because, through your research accomplishments, you are enhancing the university's reputation.

If you become a department chair, regardless of how adept you are at managing time, people, and projects, your research productivity will inevitably slow down quite a bit. Sometimes there are ways to mitigate this consequence by strictly managing your time and priorities, and other times you will be unexpectedly overwhelmed with duties that require your attention. Regardless of the scope of administrative duties, most at the department chair level maintain a research program (again, this depends upon the size of the department and expectations). Research productivity must be maintained at least at a moderate level if a chair wishes to eventually return to a faculty position.

If you have a thriving research program, you can negotiate with the university to give you additional funds to create a second-in-command position for an individual who will perpetuate your research and serve as an interface between you and the rest of the research team. Given how deep the pockets of your university might be, this could be a negotiating item. Lobbying for assistance is easier said than done, but it is a possibility worth considering. If establishing and funding this secondary role is not possible, then you must diligently manage your time while you are a department chair to continue your research. Just remember that you will not be able to travel to the number of conferences that you used to or write as many papers and proposals. Reducing your research productivity may feel frustrating, but the upside is that leading a department will become a new adventure for you.

- **Are you willing to prioritize the collective good over your personal success?** As an individual professor/researcher scaling the academic ladder, you probably experienced some adrenaline rushes as you progressed upwards (or at least some empowering accomplishments!). Things like winning millions of dollars in grants or contracts, reaching a publishing milestone of 50 or 100 papers, attending the "big" conferences in your field, and winning awards were all exciting. There is nothing wrong with enjoying any of these triumphs—as long as you keep your ego in check—but as department chair you will need to think about the collective good of the unit that you are leading rather than your personal ambitions and achievements.

  A different approach is needed when you serve as a department chair. Here is what I mean by "collective good": what types of teaching, research, and service environments can I create as department chair to help *all* the faculty succeed? The majority of your work should no longer be about writing your own proposals. Instead, you should use your time and clout to encourage and empower faculty to write proposals. There are many ways you can support these endeavors: by forming teams and providing and creating opportunities for such ventures. Here are other examples:

  – Develop initiatives and resources for faculty to travel to conferences and funding agencies to enhance their research.
  – Nominating faculty for national and international awards.

- Be aware of faculty wellbeing to avoid overloading them with service activities.
- Help faculty form partnerships and teams for proposal-writing and research ventures.
- Focus on the types and areas of research that the department should be involved in (rather than focusing on your personal research interests).

The list could be endless, but the bottom line is to focus on "us" and not on "me"!

- **Are you willing to live with some uncertainty about your future career trajectory?** You will often hear this from well-meaning peers or even mentors: "*You need to plan what the next phase of your career will look like after you finish your term as department chair.*" Let me temper those expectations by assuring you that most faculty members do not know precisely what their next steps will be. A department chair term may last for four or five years, but many circumstances are bound to change in that time frame. Some chairs may enjoy the job so much that they wish to stay for another term. Others may desire to move from chair to dean in the same organization if the opportunity presents itself (or to some other administrative position in the university). Some others leave the university to go elsewhere to another institution or into industry. Many chairs will finish a term and go right back to being a professor, relieved that they will no longer grapple with administrative concerns.

Chapter 1 Summary and Exercises

In this chapter we...

- **Discussed a variety of skills that department chairs need so they can successfully lead faculty, staff, and students.** Some prerequisite skills are pretty obvious—good time and people management, being personable, an ability to navigate processes well, etc. Other skills are less intuitive, like the capability to handle work fragmentation and how to respond to situations with emotional intelligence. I recommend that you carefully consider how you measure up in each of the categories mentioned in the chapter so that you gain a strong sense of which prerequisites you feel confident about and which ones need further development.

- **Emphasized the importance of establishing routines for maintaining your physical, mental, and emotional wellbeing.** Successful department chairs can't pour from an empty cup, so to speak. Prioritizing your personal health is perhaps the most critical aspect of ensuring that you come to work each day ready to handle whatever lands on your desk.

- **Considered the question *"Why do you want to be a department chair?"*** Every department chair candidate's response to this question will be personal and unique. And it's OK to have a variety of reasons for pursuing a job! However, tossing your application into the hat without a clear vision of why you want the job is a recipe for disaster. If you take the time to identify and articulate why you want to become a department chair, then this clarity will shine through in the application process and, ultimately, in your work as chair.

- **Discussed what could happen if you are asked to serve as interim chair.** If your previous department chair leaves and you are tapped to take on the role temporarily, it can be a great opportunity to "test drive" the job. Maybe it will end up being a great fit with your ambitions and skill sets, or maybe you will find that it isn't really for you after all. Remember that even if you serve as an interim chair, you may still need to be vetted through a formal hiring process to become the permanent chair.

Answer the following questions to learn more about how the chapter content applies to you personally.

1. In the first section of this chapter, we reviewed some of the many skill sets that a department chair must use on a daily basis. These skill sets are listed below. Use the scales below (1 = novice, 10 = master) to rate your current capabilities in these areas.

a. Time management

1   2   3   4   5   6   7   8   9   10

b. People management

1   2   3   4   5   6   7   8   9   10

c. Deadline management

1   2   3   4   5   6   7   8   9   10

d. Achieving work-life balance

1   2   3   4   5   6   7   8   9   10

e. Sociability

1   2   3   4   5   6   7   8   9   10

f. Confrontation management

1   2   3   4   5   6   7   8   9   10

g. Process management

1   2   3   4   5   6   7   8   9   10

h. Handling work fragmentation

1   2   3   4   5   6   7   8   9   10

i. Maintaining mental stamina

1   2   3   4   5   6   7   8   9   10

j. Championing initiatives

1   2   3   4   5   6   7   8   9   10

k. Demonstrating emotional intelligence

1   2   3   4   5   6   7   8   9   10

2. Based on the ratings you gave yourself, what do you think would be your biggest strengths as a department chair? What do you think you would struggle with?

3. So, why are you interested in becoming a department chair? Or if you are already on track to become a chair or are currently in the role, what originally motivated you to pursue that position?

Chapter 2.

Applying to Become a Department Chair

Assuming that you are not thrust into a department chair position on short notice, there is a deliberate way to start preparing for the job either at your current university or elsewhere. If you take some initiative in departmental activities before you apply to be a department chair, then you will gain insightful experience that will better inform you about management in academia (and will add some bonus points to your resumé).

1. **Get involved with processes.** As department chair, you must be adept at following policies, procedures, and processes. Adhering to processes is important because it keeps you and others around you out of trouble. If there is ever a grievance or a legal issue concerning your decisions or actions, you can point to the process that you followed to explain your steps and rationale. For example, a departmental policy manual is a document that every department should have and that you should consult regularly. However, some departments may neglect to update their policy manual for years at a time, and, surprisingly, some don't even bother to draft one at all. If you find yourself in the latter situation, you should take the opportunity to put one together with the assistance of your faculty and staff.

   Let's use a graduate PhD program as an example. There should be clearly written processes detailing how preliminary exams and qualifying exams are conducted. Straightforward guidelines should exist about how to construct programs of study and a host of other procedural details. If there are department committees, then there should be a clear policy on how many members serve on the committees, how they are elected, and how long their terms may last. As a faculty member, you should read and be familiar with the processes and suggest ways to improve them, if possible.

Keep in mind that there are policies written for faculty, students, and sometimes how faculty and students interact. Also, it is extremely important to make sure that department policies are not in conflict with existing policies at the college and university levels. Sometimes it may not even be necessary to write a new policy from scratch because another department may have a similar policy that you can simply modify for your department. Talk to other department chairs in your university and elsewhere; they can offer a trove of information and assistance. So, what makes a policy or process "good"? Below are some guidelines for designing solid policies.

- Policies must always be fair and equitable. They should not include biases of any sort so that everyone is equally capable of abiding by them.
- Student-related policies must be structured in an accessible, easy-to-understand format.
- Avoid tacking on exceptions, if possible. The more caveats you add to a policy or a guideline, the more ineffective it can become.

2. **Volunteer to serve** on the department strategic planning committee, or better yet, chair the committee. Getting involved in strategic planning is a good place to start when trying to better understand your department's policies, initiatives, and goals. In some universities, a self-study of the department may also be available for you to review. If not, you may have a great opportunity to lead a self-study that your current department chair will likely welcome with open arms (because one is probably long overdue). A self-study/strategic plan will outline the history of the department, the programs, statis-

tics (enrollment and retention), strengths, weaknesses, and resources available and needed.

3. **Show up at recruitment events.** If you are serious about becoming a department chair, then you need to get a sense of some of the activities that you must attend if you take on the role. Department chairs are often expected to attend recruitment events on campus and sometimes off campus to speak with potential students, parents, and others. Participating in these events will help you familiarize yourself with the recruitment machinery at your university and will give you valuable experience "selling" your university and department.

Representing your department or university at recruitment events is a great way to demonstrate commitment to your job and your employer.

4. **Host or attend an open house event.** You could demonstrate some initiative by putting together an open house in your own department for a graduate recruitment program or by participating in a university-wide graduate school open house. While your department may not have all the resources necessary to enact your vision for an open

house event, your graduate dean in your university probably has some funds allocated for this very purpose. Try coming up with a plan to increase graduate enrollment in your department. Administrators are always looking for new ideas to increase enrollment because overall success of the graduate school depends on the success levels of individual department programs. Any ideas you suggest that may benefit the university will garner the positive attention of a dean or even a provost.

5. **Get to know your dean.** The traditional chain of command to talk with your dean is always through your department chair. However, there are a few exceptions. At more casual social events you could converse with your dean about your interest in learning more about academic leadership and request some one-on-one mentoring time. Assuming that your dean is the mentoring type, this could be a great experience where you get to see perspectives from two organizational levels above your own. Deans have specific mandates on initiatives such as increasing enrollment and research expenditures. Offering your ideas and involvement will be a welcome relief for the dean who can support you in putting your plans into action and accomplishing your goals.

6. **Understand the responsibilities of your university's administrators.** As a department chair, you must learn the administrative hierarchy and some of the key personnel in the university. It's important to be aware of how decisions are made by various administrators. There is no one-size-fits-all approach when it comes to structuring universities, but typically multiple vice presidents (VPs) report to a single president. These VPs have specific functions and their own departments and staff to manage. Probably the VP with the most responsibility at your university is the VP for Academic Affairs (often called Provost) who leads the entire academic enterprise. Other VPs may include those for finance, diversity, the endowment, research, student affairs, and enrollment, among others. The provost usually

manages the various colleges in a university, and each college has a dean. As department chair, you would report to one of those deans.

Below I have shared some examples of how you could positively interact with other administrators. Keep in mind that your dean is your direct line of report, and keeping her involved is important. It is never a good idea to "go behind the back" of your dean to accomplish things. Most deans will be happy to just be kept informed of your activities (unless they are the micromanaging type).

- Graduate deans will have the deepest knowledge about graduate enrollment; therefore, they could be an ally in actions to increase the graduate enrollment in your department. Get to know how they recruit and how you can provide helpful materials and support to them.
- Often undergraduate recruitment is handled very differently and separately from graduate recruitment. Therefore, knowing which administrator is responsible for this endeavor and providing the necessary support is an important tactic in managing undergraduate enrollment in your department.
- If you are in a research-intensive department, the VP for research could be a major asset. Remember—the more research your department conducts, the more recognition your department and the entire university will receive. The VP for research can provide strategic help on diversifying your research portfolio because they normally have a wider, national sphere of influence.

It's important to know the functions of these administrators and begin to consider how you can help your university get to the next level. Also, unless you get out of your office and learn how to interact with administrators, you will not know the language of management.

7. **Learn the language of academic administration** including recruitment, retention, student success, assessment, and research productivity. Reading the strategic plan for the university will give you considerable insight into the university's goals and how they articulate

> If you are strongly interested in a department chair role at particular university, make the time to learn "who's who" in the administration. Knowing a bit about the people and the activities they lead and manage will give you a boost in the interview process. Not only will you convey that you've done your homework, but also you'll be able to ask more insightful questions.

them. It is good practice to read the last two or three versions of the strategic plan, because with every incoming president or provost, there is bound to be a new plan. Knowing the plan and how you can position your department for success in that context is essential. If you need to ask for resources like faculty positions, operating budgets, travel, etc., then aligning yourself with the strategic plan of the college and university will be vital.

8. **Read your university's strategic plan.** You know this must be important if I'm already mentioning it again! As boring as it may sound to read a massive document, this has to be done. When you read the strategic plan, pay close attention to the priorities and objectives. A good strategic plan usually includes a mission, vision, core statements, and DEI protocols. It will also contain priorities, objectives, and tactics (actions) that will be used to guide the university toward fulfilling its goals.

As department chair, you may take the helm in the middle of a strategic plan cycle. Keep in mind that as university presidents change, so will the strategic plan. If a new university-level strategic plan is being implemented when you begin as chair, then you will have a great opportunity to work with your faculty and craft a departmental plan that supports the university's mission. However, the stars rarely align for this kind of timing.

When a new dean is hired, he may be excited to draw up a strategic plan for the college that he manages. Often a new strategic plan is expected, and it can be perceived as an exercise to demonstrate the dean's leadership abilities.

Here is how one chair put it: *"I have been department chair for nearly 15 years, and I have seen three presidents come and go with each one starting a strategic planning exercise. It was the same thing over and over. One wanted a top-down approach, and another wanted a ground-up approach. It was exhausting because they wanted so much information from the department chairs. To make matters even more challenging, I have seen two deans during my tenure as chair. The first one quickly recognized the pervasive strategic planning fatigue, but the other dean wanted to design a college-level strategic plan. It took all my discipline to not scream at myself in the mirror."*

While strategic plans provide important road maps for both short- and long-term planning for a university, faculty can only get on board with a plan if the priorities and objectives are carefully implemented. It's one thing to say that the university wants to achieve a top ten ranking nationwide for its psychology program, but if there are no appropriate investments to move towards that goal, frustration can set in easily amongst faculty. Many will roll their eyes and see it as an exercise in futility. I have met several senior faculty members across universities who have endured numerous strategic planning exercises. It can be an exhausting process because a lot of data must be collected, and, in the end, a consulting firm hired by the university will report many things that they already know.

9. **Get to know other department chairs** in your college and university. Most chairs would love the opportunity to go out for lunch to talk about their jobs. I suggest that you keep encounters informal and not "grill" them too hard, as though it were an interview. Have discussions about challenges and things they like and don't like about their positions. Often some patterns will begin to emerge. If you want

to lead your department, engaging in conversations with seasoned chairs will help you mold your expectations. Be warned that some chairs are perennial whiners, though, and nothing can ever satisfy them. Take their attitudes with a grain of salt, but look for consistent patterns, especially if there are many department chairs in your college that seem disgruntled.

10. **Get to know your stakeholders.** A stakeholder is "a person with an interest or concern in something, especially a business." Depending on which university you are associated with, there may be a scarcity or a plethora of stakeholders. Usually, the primary stakeholders that people think about in a university setting are financial donors. They want to invest or give funds to a program or department because they believe in the work of the faculty and the community in which it is embedded. For example, a top ten corporation in the area may want to fund student scholarships to educate the next generation while also building a pipeline to their organization. Other stakeholders want to attach their name to the prestige of a university or an individual within the university. There are some departments that may collaborate with government agencies that want to fund research, students, and scientists, and others to support the research mandate of their organization. Being aware of stakeholders, their needs, and how to work with them is a key aspect of being a successful department chair.

11. **Assess the university budget.** As a top-notch researcher or just someone who has always been good with budgets and finances, you may know how to operate at the faculty level. If you are a researcher who manages multiple grants and contracts, you will be familiar with the process of assembling a budget. You understand salary structures, operating expenses, overhead (taxes!), operating expenses, subcontracts, and other line items. You probably even have a system in place (or have a program coordinator) to calculate spending levels and know how to carefully plan for the year and the funding cycles.

    However, when you become a department chair, some of these "clear-cut" ways of dealing with budgetary matters will become more nuanced. You will likely have to deal with unexpected, complicated issues and work with a budget that is not large enough to address all the concerns of the department. If you have active research faculty in the department who have large budgets, consider yourself fortunate, because they are not interested in asking you for funding for travel or other expenses that are covered by grants. On the other hand, just because these faculty members do not ask for funds does not mean that you should not engage in meaningful conversations about their needs and how you can help them realize their goals. Most research faculty will appreciate that gesture.

If you have faculty who depend on the university to foot the bill for conferences, purchase computers and equipment, and provide graduate students to support their research and teaching, then you need to have a plan in place to provide a fair and equitable way to distribute funds. If you are in college where budgets are limited, then you have to balance this carefully. One hand you have faculty who want "a lot," and on the other hand you have a dean who is only willing to allocate limited funds for your department. Your dean may clearly state that if your faculty want funds to travel, they have to write and win proposals to funding agencies. In response, your faculty will likely push you to advocate more for your department.

Navigating this situation is a difficult part of serving as department chair. While you should advocate for your department to secure funds for your faculty, you must also challenge and provide opportunities for faculty to write proposals to obtain outsourced funding. Sharing strategic ideas with your faculty about how they can increase their chances of winning proposals will go a long way toward cementing your leadership skills in your department. If you are tired of hearing your dean say "no", then you can always roll up your sleeves and pursue fundraising opportunities for your department. Just because your dean cannot fund initiatives does not mean that another stakeholder will not fund your ideas.

I know of a department chair who was tired of hearing his dean say "no" or "we don't have funds" for a study abroad program in Central America. The chair was either unable to convince the dean, or the dean was not interested in such initiatives. But he did not give up. He took this plan to the Vice President for Research, wrote a short report of what this would mean for the university and highlighted potential "return on investment" scenarios, and prepared a short presentation. After several discussions, the VPR was on board with the program. She funded the initiative, and it became a huge success in the university. This success was made possible because the chair sought ways to externally fund the program. Thinking outside the box—especially when it comes to funds—is of paramount importance for a department chair. You can either throw up your hands in surrender or do the hard work of figuring out ways to fund important initiatives.

12. **Write a mock vision plan.** If you are department chair or aspire to be one, writing a "vision plan" is an excellent exercise to define your ideas and priorities about academic leadership. Don't delegate the work of writing a plan to a committee of faculty members. Seek their input, but it should be your job to write and communicate a vision with enthusiasm and excellence. Just about every good leadership book will tell you that a clear vision that is communicated regularly is important for motivating a team. A vision plan should be ambitious and should discuss the plans to become a superior department by striving for innovative teaching methods, first-class research, and engagement with the community. Here's how one chair put it: *"Oftentimes in the rush to increase enrollment, retention, and research revenue, universities forget that the main goal is to provide an excellent education to our students who will go on to become successful in their careers. Their success means the university garners a good reputation."* Well said!

13. **Read academic leadership books.** As discussed previously, most universities do an unimpressive job of training and mentoring the next generation of leaders. Others address this responsibility haphazardly by having a few seminars and asking potential candidates to go through some mundane exercises. Others, in their eagerness to check a box, hire a consultant to come and conduct a day-long workshop.

There are no shortcuts if universities want to invest in their employees to become future leaders. There ought to be dedicated programs that diligently and thoroughly mentor individuals. Therefore, reading administrative books is extremely useful. I think several particularly useful books have been published, but you may find some more helpful than others. I suggest that you check for relevant books at your university's library or simply purchase them. Read, take good notes, and pass them along to the next person.

Reading books about academic leadership helps you prepare to step into a leadership role.

The application process

Applying for the department chair position should not be done on a whim. It should be a well thought out process complete with an excellent cover letter, a tailored resumé, and references that speak to your strengths. Before I became a department chair (in the same university where I had been a professor), I insisted that there be a formal interview process with requirements to write a position statement and converse with faculty, students, and other stakeholders. These components lent legitimacy to the vetting process and compelled me to ponder various aspects of the department chair position. Here are some things to consider as you begin the application process.

- Read the job announcement carefully, especially if the department chair position is at another university. It may be useful to contact the chair of the search committee to gather additional details and ask questions.
- It is essential to ensure that your credentials match the job description. There's no sense in applying for the job if you do not have the required skills and qualifications.
- Read a book on academic leadership (at least one!). Though I will stop short of fully endorsing certain books, I will say that there are many excellent ones on the market. (Check out Appendix C for a list of possible resources.)
- Do some research on the department that has captured your interest (if you are not already a member of the department). If you can gain access to the department's strategic plan, be sure to read it thoroughly, then tailor your cover letter/position statement to carefully align your strengths with the plan.
- Choose references who will highlight your strengths but are also candid about your abilities.

Department chair application processes may differ among universities, but there are usually a few important documents that you will be required to submit.

1. **Curriculum Vitae (CV).** Your CV should be an organized, thorough document that outlines your education, professional journey, research, teaching, notable accomplishments, and any awards. It will not be sufficient to simply turn in a list of peer-reviewed papers, grants, and contracts along with your education and work profiles. On a CV, your education and employment history must be chronicled properly, and professional formatting should be applied to your list of peer-reviewed papers, grants, and contracts. Descriptions of awards should also be included to help readers better understand their significance.

   Perhaps what most candidates do not include in their CV is their experience in managing and leading people. If you have a large research portfolio, only listing your papers, grants, and dollar values are not enough. It will also be important to briefly discuss your leadership role as part of these efforts. Your CV provides a prime opportunity to articulate how your research and teaching accomplishments illustrate your management and leadership capabilities. Finally, it is critical to ensure that your CV is as comprehensive as possible because this document may also be referenced during your promotion/tenure process. Therefore, the courses you have taught, students you have supervised, and committees you have served on (with corresponding dates) should all be included on your CV.

2. **Cover letter.** A cover letter is usually how you connect your CV to the job description of the department chair. Your cover letter should communicate the excitement you have for the job and your willingness to lead the department. It is your responsibility to showcase your knowledge, skills, abilities, and other traits in your cover letter in a way that convinces readers that you are a natural fit for the position. Make sure to highlight key aspects of the job description and explain how they align with your portfolio. While this is not the place to be "shy" about your awards and abilities, neither is it the place to appear "pompous"

to the point faculty and administration may hesitate in asking you to come for an interview. I have seen cover letters where candidates go so far as to write a short strategic plan for the department. Be careful not to overstep in advocating for change because you do not know all the factors that must be considered for that particular department.

A polished cover letter can help you make a strong first impression.

3. **Tenure and promotion application.** If you are currently a professor and have climbed the academic ladder from assistant to associate to full professor, you have already gone through various processes at each transition stage. However, if you apply for a department chair job at another university, your application that includes a CV, cover letter, and position paper may not be enough. The process at the university at which you are applying may require you to go through an additional "tenure and promotion to professor" process. Don't feel insulted or take it personally if the university requires this step; it may just be their standard policy. Usually, your application package for department chair will also be used for the tenure and promotion process. In other cases, a bit more may be required, such as a "justification for tenure and promotion statement." All documents will be reviewed by faculty in the department, the college, and possibly a university review board.

4. **References.** If your application asks for a list of references, then it is imperative that you provide that in the appropriate place in your application materials. Think carefully about who knows you well (professionally), has perpetually supported you, and is a good communicator. Your references should always be people who have your best interest at heart. Do yourself a favor and make sure that you let your references know ahead of time that they may be contacted regarding your applications. A university calling one of your references unawares is not the kind of situation you want to create.

5. **Position paper.** Some universities may require you to write a position paper that may include your vision for the department and why you think you are a good fit to be a department chair. It may not even be called a position paper in the application process, but what they really want to know is why you think you are a good fit for the department. Even if the application process does not require one, it is an excellent idea to go through the exercise of writing a position paper. What kinds of credentials, experience, and strengths do you have to offer? What is your vision, and where do you see the department in the next 5 to 10 years? Parts of what you produce can be included in a cover letter, and I'm sure it will come in handy when you sit down for an interview. (Pro trip: be sure to re-read your cover letter and position paper before your interview so you are familiar with their contents.)

   I often find that department chairs and other administrators who write the most impressive cover letters and give the best interviews are the ones who have read books on academic administrative leadership and are willing to look for wisdom on how to lead people. Preparation is key, and reading books and pertinent literature will help you draft and fine-tune your cover letter and position paper. These actions will also help you prepare for tough interview questions. In the next few pages, I've shared the position paper that I wrote when I applied for the department chair position in 2010 for the Department of Atmospheric Science at the University of Alabama in Huntsville (UAH).

Position paper supporting my candidacy for department chair

Sundar A. Christopher
Professor, Department of Atmospheric Science (ATS)
Associate Director, Earth System Science Center (ESSC)
The University of Alabama in Huntsville
Huntsville, AL

At the risk of starting this document in a negative tone, writing a position paper to support my candidacy for the chair of the Department of Atmospheric Science seems rather awkward. After all, most if not all 'position papers' have a question mark attached to the end of a statement and are often an arguable opinion about an issue. In this case, I would have to title my paper as 'Why should I become a department chair?' or worse still 'Why am I qualified to become a department chair?' I chose not to write such a position paper but instead provide the reader some details on my background, some musings on the chair's position, and some ideas on what I would like to accomplish.

First, I want to thank the ATS faculty for unanimously nominating me for the chair's position. My conversations with you indicate that your expectations are high, and we need to work collectively to move our department forward!

Before I write any further, it is important that the reader knows something about my background and my path that led me to this stage. I came to the United States from India in 1987 to get a master's degree in Atmospheric Science at South Dakota School of Mines and Technology (SDSMT). I then went to Colorado State University to finish my Ph.D., and I was hired as an Assistant Professor at SDSMT for a brief period until I came to UAHuntsville—some 12 years ago. My research interests are primarily in satellite remote sensing, but judging by the breadth of my peer-reviewed papers over the last 10 years, I have diversified my portfolio to stay competitive and to explore new areas.

I started my career at UAHuntsville in 1997 as an Assistant Professor, was promoted to Associate Professor in 2001, granted tenure in 2002, and promoted to Full Professor in 2007. I was also appointed as the Associate Director of the Earth System Science Center primarily to work with NOAA on positioning UAHuntsville for a national Cooperative Institute.

For those of you who are into numbers, this section is for you! I have published about 75 papers in peer-reviewed journals and a lot more than that in conference publications/presentations (we really don't keep track of conference publications in our discipline since they are not peer-reviewed). In 2006, my peers voted for me to receive UAHuntsville's highest research award—the Research and Creative Achievement Award. I single out that accomplishment amongst others because of the peer recognition at UAHuntsville. Plus, it came with a $2500 check! Currently, I manage nearly a dozen grants and a research team of about 10-12 including students and research scientists. More recently, we published 15 peer-reviewed papers in 2008. That is a testimony to the hard work of my research team. I have won more than $7M in funded research, and I have graduated more than a dozen students with M.S/Ph.D. Several of my students are winners of NASA's prestigious Earth Science Fellowship awards, and two of them are now Assistant Professors at major Universities in the nation. I have been asked to serve on climate change panels and numerous science and satellite teams for NASA. I have designed and taught more than 6 graduate courses and one undergraduate course. I have also been invited to speak at national and international venues including the United Nations Symposium on Space Applications in Austria and the World Federation of Scientists in Sicily. As my chair, Dean, and Provost can vouch for, I have served and continue to serve on various University committees. I have been involved in various departmental committees including course scheduling, tenure evaluation, and also served as 'acting' chair for short periods of time. Gory details are in the attached CV.

The list of duties for the chair in the UAHuntsville faculty handbook is daunting! As Walter Gmelch, a leading authority on academic leadership puts it—the chair is caught in the godlike role of Janus, a Roman

God with two faces, looking in two directions at the same time, swiveling between their faculty colleagues and the University administration. To balance these roles, Gmelch recommends that the chair must learn to swivel without appearing dizzy, schizophrenic, or 'two-faced'. Therein lies the challenge! Obviously, if I were to view the academic department as a first-order closed system, the primary constituents for a chair are the students, the faculty, and the administration. In an open system, this includes the local community, media, sponsors, collaborators, and a host of other individuals, organizations, and communities. I expect to be fully involved with all aspects of this open system.

The graduate program in ATS has garnered a top-ten ranking in a short period of time. The program is hardly 15 years old, and this ranking is a testimony to the hard work of the faculty, staff, and students. The program currently has about 60+ students, and most of them are supported by full-time Graduate Research Assistantships. The newly started (2008) undergraduate program in Earth System Science (ESS) has an exciting growth potential provided the correct mix of courses, resources, support, and enthusiasm is available. It also appears that this could grow into a master's and a Ph.D. level program.

The long-term success of any graduate and undergraduate program will always be judged by the success of the students who take on leadership roles in the research and larger community. Therefore, significant investment needs to be placed on providing high quality education coupled with a research focus that is meaningful to a larger audience. I envision our students to take their places in the worldwide community as leaders, researchers, educators, policy makers, business owners, and in various other arenas. Students have been an important focus of my career. That is one of the reasons I teach a Professional Development course for students and travel the country giving seminars to empower students to become successful. If all goes well, my first ever book should be coming out this year that is titled—'Positioning yourself for success—A career guide for graduate students and a must read for every advisor'.

It is no secret that the ATS department is among the leaders in research productivity at UAHuntsville. The faculty members are leaders in their respective research areas and have been highly successful in winning external funding from various agencies. The NSSTC where the ATS department is housed has excellent collaborative potential. One of my goals is to foster collaborations with the National Weather Service. For example, ATS can develop a customer-based curriculum that will enable our students to find employment within the NWS and broadcast meteorology sectors. The NASA Earth Science Division at NSSTC has been a strong supporter of the ATS program. With high quality student applicants for the ATS graduate program, we need to be working closely with NASA Principal Investigators and scientists. The USRA within NSSTC is another asset. As ATS chair, it is my goal to provide high quality graduate and undergraduate students to work with the USRA researchers. We need to think broadly about customer needs to develop and strengthen students in the focus areas that will secure good employment for them.

Since I always ask my students to list out Strengths, Weakness, Opportunities, and Threats (SWOT), I would be remiss if I did not include mine in this paper. My strengths include organizational capabilities and the ability to manage multiple projects effectively. I have built solid research and professional relationships with several individuals within and outside NSSTC. I manage nearly a dozen grants, teach, write papers, conduct research, and fiercely guard my racquetball appointments! I am a mentor to students, young faculty here and elsewhere and I find that portion of my job highly rewarding. As chair of ATS and the Associate Director of ESSC, I will have the ability to combine the strengths of a research center and an academic department that can foster further collaborative research and provide leading edge courses to the students. As for weaknesses, even though I have been at UAHuntsville, I have to learn the budgetary process of 'running a department'. As a Principal Investigator, I am used to having full control of the budgets of my grants and contracts. Therefore, I have to learn the ropes of administrative budgets and how to work with the Dean to fulfill College of Science goals that are in line with the UAHuntsville vision. It is my opinion that a chair must manage, lead, develop faculty, and maintain scholarship. I've always taught and trained students and my research team using a 'hands-on' approach. I intend to be fully engaged in my scholarship activities of writing papers and proposals, and therefore, I will rely heavily on administrative staff to delegate responsibilities.

The opportunities are plenty to move the department forward. The awareness on the earth's environment, weather, and climate are high, and the anthropogenic impact on these factors are being studied through both inter and multidisciplinary approaches. Therefore, opportunities for growth are tremendous through collaboration within departments, centers, across campus, other Universities, and other organizations. The threats and challenges are also huge. For a department to grow from one level to another requires resources. Resources for new faculty, infrastructure, recruitment, and a host of other needs are required. Balancing these threats against opportunities is critical, especially if one requires the chair to lead. Nothing could be more frustrating to the chair and the faculty to have vision but inadequate resources and support to fulfill the goals that are required to make the Atmospheric and Earth System Science programs among the premier units in the country! Together with the Dean and the administration, I am prepared to chart out a course that maximizes strengths, mitigates weakness, and leverages such opportunities that exist—without getting frustrated!

To gain further momentum and to take the ATS into the top 5 in our nation will require some careful and diligent planning. This requires the ATS faculty and the chair to work closely with the Dean, Provost, and the President to accomplish these goals. The chair must work with the faculty to be more involved in national and international committees. Active, focused recruiting is highly important to obtain highly qualified students. ATS will require resources to hire new faculty to strengthen the graduate and undergraduate programs. The chair must create opportunities for the students to participate on national committees and work with our partners in NSSTC. We must seek to obtain resources for student fellowships and postdoctoral scientists. Even as I am wrapping up this position paper, I am in the process of submitting a proposal (with NASA MSFC partners) as part of the 'stimulus package' to NASA HQ— to request graduate student fellowships in Earth Sciences that will bridge the gap between Research and Applications. The opportunities are plenty!

As a final thought, I believe that while the challenges are immense, so is the growth potential. The faculty and students of the ATS and ESS are among the best in the nation, and collectively we can move this department forward.

Sincerely,
Sundar A. Christopher
Professor, Atmospheric Science
Associate Director, Earth System Science Center

Interviewing for the position

Interviewing builds considerable discipline. Careful preparation, study, and practice are required to develop this skill, and it's not unusual to invest many hours getting ready for the experience. Believe it or not, preparing for an interview should be a bit exciting!

Even if you are going to lead the department where you are currently working as a professor, don't settle for simply being appointed to the position without due process. Insist that the standards applied to external candidates be applied to you as well. You should fulfill all the steps—submit a cover letter, CV, and position paper, give a seminar on your vision, talk to faculty, students, and the dean, etc. This gives your desire for the position a lot of credibility. It also clearly signals to the faculty that you are serious about doing this job well.

If you apply to become a department chair at another institution, you will almost certainly be required to follow a standard procedure. The job announcement will likely specify the process. After you clear the application hurdles, you will likely be invited to an "airport interview" and then an on-campus interview. But there could be many variations to these steps, especially if the department is screening candidates via phone or video calls.

The airport interview (initial interview). Depending upon the university, if you are an external candidate, you could be asked to fly to the airport closest to the university to take part in a preliminary interview. Phone or video conferencing interviews have become increasingly common in lieu of in-person preliminary interviews, though. This is the stage where the university is down-selecting from the applicant pool. If a university receives 25 applications for the chair position, the review committee's first responsibility will be to down-select this group to maybe 7-10 strong candidates. Usually only three or four candidates may be invited to the campus for a final interview, so the committee uses the "airport interview" to whittle the pool down even further.

So, dress appropriately (like you want to be a department chair), and if you are invited to a video conference interview, make sure that you have a good camera and microphone and an appropriate visual background. Set up in a quiet, well-lit space, and don't let your cat or dog or child wander through the camera during your interview! All these details may matter to your committee and convey to them how seriously you are taking the application process.

No matter how adorable they are, job interviews are not the time for your pets to make an appearance!

Initial interviews are always a simple probing experience. The committee wants to know if you can communicate effectively and if you can clearly answer the interview questions that they pose. Some of these interviews are very structured. All candidates may get the same questions so the committee can rate and rank each candidate's responses to help them form a short list of on-campus interview candidates. Others may see some deviation depending upon how you respond to certain questions.

Your goal is to appear confident in your credentials, experience, strengths, and even in your weaknesses. If you do not know the answer to a question, it is better to say "I'm not sure" than to say something totally wrong or inappropriate. For example, if you have no idea how to address, assess, and champion DEI measures, it is better to say that you do not know rather than attempt to parrot something you may have heard someone say years ago. It is a complex topic and should be studied and thought about in great depth, so a one-dimensional answer will reveal much about your lack of preparation. At the end, they will give you an opportunity to ask questions. Be sure to ask pertinent questions about the department and not something controversial such as "Tell me something about the interpersonal conflicts you have in your department?" or worse still, "Who are the troublemakers in your department?" You think I am kidding, correct? Nope. Having served in a few administrative positions myself, I know that interviews can be interesting and surprising at times!

The campus interview. This is the most important interview in the whole process. You got through several major hurdles, and now you are up against the best few candidates. Of course, you do not know who the other candidates are, unless you are an internal candidate. Yes, this happens sometimes. This situation arises when the university where you work wants to conduct a national search for a new department chair, and they want to make sure that the same application process is available to all existing faculty in the department. This provides a good equal opportunity framework.

There are some advantages and some disadvantages to being an internal candidate. One definite advantage is that you will know the identities of the other candidates and even get to listen in on their presentations. You can assess your competition this way! Another advantage is that you are familiar with the inner workings of your department, college, and the university. This does not automatically mean that you will be chosen as the next department chair. It is often easier for a department chair to come from the outside to lead a faculty group because there is no preexisting "she is one of *ours*" bias. An external hire will likely have more objectivity when reviewing policies and practices, and a fresh, new perspective is sometimes just what a department needs.

A complex aspect of being department chair is that you must operate in both an external- and internal-facing position. By "external-facing," I mean that you are the "face" of the department to the outside world, including your own university. You are expected to interact with the dean, office of admissions, office of research, human resources department, and various other groups and administrators on campus. Therefore, the interview process must showcase that you can deal with various constituencies with care. To that end, choosing your words wisely is crucial during the interview process. Slang words (cool, nifty, baloney), inappropriate words (you know what those are), and colloquialisms (y'all, gonna) that could be misinterpreted by or offend some individuals must be avoided. Speak clearly and concisely, and never monopolize conversations. A university president once told me that was impressed by the credentials of a person who was interviewing for department chair, but the president could hardly get in a word edgewise during the whole one-hour discussion! Needless to say, the candidate was not selected. Little things matter.

The dinner. You should be prepared to be invited to dinner with a few faculty members, committee members, staff, administrators, and possibly the current department chair who is either finishing a term or an interim. Dinner is usually when the casual conversations happen and where everyone around the table can get a sense of the "social you." It is not only an opportunity for the committee to get to know you in a less formal setting but also for you to get to know your potential colleagues and the university a bit better. Be careful that you don't form impressions of the entire department or university from a subset of members comprising your dinner companions. I am often asked the specifics of what to eat and drink and what to expect. My suggestion is to keep it simple. Don't order things that are ridiculously expensive (it's rarely ever a good idea to order the most expensive thing on the menu!), difficult to eat in public (nix the spaghetti order), or alcoholic (especially if it's going to make you a bit looser with words). Also, go easy on the dessert if most folks are not ordering any.

The important people you will meet. You should expect to meet the dean and, in most cases, the provost as well—after all they are the academic chain of command. Depending on the profile of the department, the president of the university may want to meet you as well. Of course, lunch with other department chairs in the college and research staff is often obligatory. Hopefully you were sent an itinerary before you arrived so you have an idea of what will occur during your visit. Below I've listed the people with whom you will most likely meet and a little about why each is important.

- **Staff assistant/administrative assistant.** If you do not see time budgeted for meeting the staff assistant/administrative assistant on the itinerary, make it a priority to request at least one hour to speak with him or her. This is a person that you will be working with on a regular basis, so getting to know this person and hearing his or her thoughts about how the department currently operates is vital information.

- **Dean.** The dean is looking to see if she can work with you and understand your personality. How clearly you articulate your ideas will also be important to her. I even had a provost mention to me one time he considered how "polished" a candidate appeared to be! Meeting with the dean is an opportunity to ask chair-like questions about where the college is headed and her perspectives on your department's role within the university. Be sure to ask some open-ended questions, such as "What are some of the challenges that the department is facing?" You never know the answer you might get. Better yet, ask "From your vantage point, what do you perceive to be the strengths and weaknesses of the department?" Take good mental notes, and see if some of the dean's comments line up with the rest of the interview.

- **"Big wigs."** Expect to speak with the provost, research staff, graduate dean, and possibly even the university president. To prepare for these interviews and discussions, you must "do your homework" before you arrive on campus. Review the university's web page diligently, and be familiar with the vision of the college. You may have only 30 minutes to speak with these busy administrators. Make the best of it.

- **Current department chair.** This will probably be a closed-door session where the outgoing chair will want to offer words of wisdom. Again, listen carefully, because depending upon the chairperson, the conversation could be realistic, positive, or downright depressing. It is reasonable to ask what the chair thinks about the status of the operating budget, faculty course loads, and the general morale of the department. Ask the chair what he thinks will be upcoming challenges the department might face soon. It is also reasonable to ask what expectations the dean has of the chair's function. Again, strike a good balance in this conversation as you gently probe the affairs of the department. You should allow the chair to talk as freely as he can because his comments may be particularly illuminating. It is quite possible that the chair may be leaving on difficult terms, so anything that the chair says that is excessively negative must be interpreted with caution.

- **Students.** It is always a rewarding experience to talk with students. Rather than presenting a set of slides to them, it is often a good idea to simply relax and prompt them to ask questions. In the beginning, you may have to urge them a bit to get them talking, but talking about your journey from a student to a department chair candidate will "personalize" you. However, be genuine and voice your expectations for high standards, but leave them with the fact that you will support them as you motivate them.

- **Provost and President.** Meeting with administrators on the provost and president levels will be an executive discussion where they will probably discuss large initiatives, campus projects, the need to increase enrollment, research status, improving research funding, etc. I knew a president of a university who could not talk about anything other than the new buildings (capital projects) he was working on! Sometimes presidents do forget that department chairs and other administrators cannot relate much to capital projects because they are working in the trenches of daily administration. Be ready to talk about some of your ideas to take the department to the next level.

  Listen carefully, and ask questions that help you interpret how the upper echelon of administrators view the dean, current chairperson, and faculty. Often you will note a mismatch amongst these voices, but that is normal in most places, as long as it is not completely divergent. If the dean has told you that you will be expected to recruit three new faculty members, and if the provost or president tells you that there will not be any new faculty positions for the next two years, then there is clearly a lack of communication and shared vision between these administrative levels. Wisely glean information from what these administrators have to say, and refrain from telling the president of the university, "But the dean this morning said…"

The debrief. In most universities, at the end of the one- or multi-day interview process, the dean is usually the one to provide a debrief. Keep in mind that the dean may not have had a chance to gather all the necessary feedback, so this is usually not the time to start talking about salary and other negotiations. The dean will provide a short overview of the people you have met and tell you what to expect next. Unless you are the only candidate being interviewed (which is rare), no final statements about whether you have the job will be made. At the end, the dean may ask if there are any other items that you'd like to discuss.

I have seen a wide variety of ways in which these discussions go. Some department chair candidates talk about the "two-body" problem: their spouse will also need employment at the university. Some universities' human resources departments may have the ability to handle such situations, but often the dean cannot resolve the "two-body" problem. But at least she knows about your request if you tell her and will hopefully do her best to accommodate. It is possible a timeline for the process will be outlined and that the dean expects the candidate who is selected to start June 1 (as an example). Everyone understands that there are obligations that you have at your home university and that a transition time will be required. Make sure that you ask any relevant questions about timeline and expectations in this debriefing session before you say your final goodbyes!

Department resources and job negotiation matters

Sometimes, imagining what it will be like to be a department chair may conjure grandiose notions of an unlimited budget to plan and execute a vision, a multitude of staff to help with your day-to-day work, a lot of discretionary funding for travel, and fancy furniture for your huge office. Some department chairs that I have interviewed also desire the authority to hire many new faculty in the department. There is nothing wrong with having a list of wants and a set of expectations, but you should temper these anticipations with reality. First, let's focus on one of the most important factors you will deal with as department chair: the budget.

Department budget. You need to begin with a clear understanding of the department's resources so you have realistic expectations of what you can accomplish and what may be out of reach. Usually, you will not be given this depth of information during the interview stage, but you can ask general questions when you meet with the dean or the current department chair. It is reasonable to ask how the department operating budget functions—is it set by the dean? or does it have to be negotiated each academic (or fiscal) year? What types of discretionary funds are available for the department chair to implement initiatives? Does the chair need to ask the dean's permission for certain types of purchases? One chair I spoke with described how they often felt shortchanged by the dean's budgeting plan.

"As chair, one of the things that really frustrated me was the fact that the dean never engaged in any meaningful discussions about how the operating budget was to be set for the academic year. He always said something vague like—it is based on historical spending and allocations. The dean then allotted a meager sum of money that could hardly make ends meet in the department. Worse still for major purchases and even travel, as chair

I had to 'ask' the dean. It felt like I was always given an allowance that I could not manage because the dean had huge expectations for increasing enrollment, research productivity, and such."

I am sure that some of you reading this can relate to this scenario. When I served as dean, I made it very clear that I would engage in discussions with department members early in the budget planning process to determine the sum of money that a department would need for the next year. With the total amount settled upfront, this allowed the chairs to have full control of the dollars, and they did not have to request special approval for purchases. They also knew that once that sum of money was sent to the department, I usually did not entertain additional requests for dollars, unless an unexpected and serious set of circumstances arose. The department chairs loved this format because they felt they could manage their budgets with fiscal authority.

*Avoid allowing your budget dollars to
be redistributed for other purposes.*

No matter how carefully you plan department spending, there will sometimes be money remaining in the operating departmental account at the end of the fiscal year. If the funds can be rolled over into the next fiscal year, you get to keep the money and develop some initiatives—terrific! However, it is always tempting for the dean to absorb leftover dollars back into her account.

One chair said, *"I usually knew when I was going to have funds leftover in the current academic year's budget, and I also knew that at the end of the fiscal year, a giant sweep would happen and all of that was going to be absorbed by the dean. So, I would spend all the funds in the current fiscal year by buying things that sometimes I really did not need—simply because I knew the funds would vanish. I really wish they could have left the money in the account so I could carry it over to the next year to develop some faculty/student initiatives. But that was the system, and I figured out a way to maximize the department's benefits through the system."*

Another chair also lamented being forced to relinquish funds. *"I hated to give back the money because I felt that it was not fair, so I painted some walls in the department, upgraded computers (even though they were not needed), and bought some high-end furniture."* I am quite sure that some of you reading this book who are already department chairs are in a similar situation. The eagerness to make someone clear the books just for accounting purposes creates a lot of frustration and waste.

Departmental budgets can become very complex. Managing a department budget is quite different from managing research dollars. Research funds are typically budgeted based on the proposal or statement of work, and very little deviation is allowed. Salary dollars were to be spent on salaries, travel dollars on travel, etc. You could not take all the travel dollars and start hiring more graduate research assistants. Major changes to the original budgetary allotments would require permission from various entities. This is accountability in action. We will discuss budgets in detail later in the book, but you have to realize that there may already be a system in place that dictates how the dean doles out operating budgets for departments. Therefore, at least for the first year, you may not have the ability to make additional requests. However, after you gain some experience with the operating budget, you will be in a better position to advocate financially for your department.

You can read more about how to manage department budgets in chapter 3, but now let's shift focus to other characteristics of the department chair role. The day-to-day experiences and expectations of being a department chair may vary considerably from university to university, so it's vital to have a clear idea of what you're stepping into from day 1. Discussed below are some questions to ask, preferably before you accept a chair position.

- **Am I expected to teach courses?** Depending on the size of the department, the expectations, and the culture, you may be required to teach at least one course per semester. In some cases, department chairs are only administrators with no teaching responsibilities. Whether it's required or not, my advice is to continue teaching at least one class. Faculty in your department will respect you more if you teach—call it leading by example—because it signals that you will take action to stay in touch with the needs of the department and with students. Keeping one foot "in the trenches" makes you seem relatable and reliable, plus, teaching really does keep you clued into how students are faring. I even know some deans who continue to teach one course every year or two. Given the complexity of a dean's job, that is a huge commitment that should be applauded. In the managing up and the managing down processes, teaching signifies to the faculty that you are not just an administrator, and you are interested in understanding the current, relevant issues of academics in the department. You can tell your faculty to increase student success and retention, but they will respect you far more and become invested in your goals for the department if you grapple with the same issues that they may face—students not coming to class, turning in their work late, or not going to the tutoring/success center.

- **How will my research be impacted?** Your research has been a central part of your career path, so it's critical to fully understand how it may be affected if you become chair. Remember, depending upon the size of your department, it may be difficult to manage departmental affairs and devote time to research. If you are a strong researcher with funded grants/contracts and several undergraduates, graduate students, and post-docs on your team or in your lab, then you will be expected to continue a certain level of research. In my opinion, a research-active chair lends strength to the chair position because it signals to everyone that you want to maintain your research productivity and that you have high expectations for their productivity as well. Again, leading by example is the advisable way to go, and after your term ends as department chair, you can more easily transition back to significant research activities. If you give up research completely, it is almost impossible to jumpstart your research program after you finish your term as chair if you decide to resume your status as a faculty member.

- **Will there be space for my research team members?** If you are moving from one university to another, it is quite possible that some of your research team members will be interested in moving with you. These team members are probably fully supported by your research grants and contracts. Some of your graduate students may also be interested in transferring with you to the new university. Depending on the size of your team, this should be a serious negotiation item, and you should insist that specifics about office and lab spaces are spelled out in your offer letter. I hate to say this, but verbal agreements in most academic organizations are not particularly reliable. From the time you negotiate your job perks with administrators to the time you arrive on campus, changes in leadership may occur, causing verbal agreements to be forgotten or dismissed as non-binding. This could be a huge source of frustration, because you may find that the spaces you were promised for offices and labs are no longer what you are being offered.

    While we are discussing moving teams, you may also find yourself in a situation where one or more of your graduate students at your current university have not finished either their master's or PhD degrees under your supervision. I'll assume that these students are being supported by your grants and contracts. After you have accepted the job offer, you should set up a meeting to discuss options with your students. Students at the master's level usually spend only two or three years in a program. If a student is close to graduating, it is best to continue to establish funding even after you plan to leave the university so there is continuity for the student. At that point, you need to work with the department chair at your current university to appoint a chair for the student's committee, and it is important that you continue to serve as a committee member on the committee to see her through. Graduate students who have just begun their program may want to re-enroll at your new university and transfer the appropriate credits. Unless a PhD student is very close to completion, it may be best that they move to the new university with you, unless other situations (family, finances, and other commitments) prevent them from doing so. Transferring courses and programs of study from one university to another is non-trivial and involves clear communication and cooperation between the graduate schools at both universities. Prepare yourself and your transferring students for potential bumps in the road in this process because many graduate schools are very rigid in how courses are transferred due to established rules and policies and also accreditation standards.

- **What are the fundraising expectations?** Raising funds for your department may be stipulated as part of your duties as chair or not. Either way, relying on your university to provide funds for all your initiatives is not always advisable. Seeking ways to raise your own funds means that you can develop your own initiatives to move your department forward more quickly. I know a department chair who was never given a budget to host a reception at an annual conference. The chair worked with a local industry to obtain funds, involved the industry partner in the reception, and conducted a successful reception that raised the visibility of the department. Guess what—the next year, the dean and other administrators wanted to pitch in towards the reception, because everyone wants their name associated with a successful group. The administrators followed through with providing funds to create an even more successful event the following year.

If you are harboring an intent to become a dean at a later stage in your career, raising funds at the department chair level will elevate your application. Deans, in general, are considered CEOs of their college and are expected to raise significant funds. Therefore, flexing your fundraising muscles as department chair can only serve you well. A word of caution though—it is good practice to check with your office of endowment (the office that is responsible for raising funds for the entire university) before you start contacting potential donors. Why so? Because if the endowment office has been developing a relationship with an industry partner or donor for a while to request a multimillion-dollar gift, you will be stepping on their toes. Plus, the potential donor will think that the university does not have a well-coordinated plan to coordinate gifts to the university.

- **How will I be evaluated each year?** Every university has a process for evaluating department chairs. Usually, it is an annual process in which the dean speaks with the faculty and personnel that the chair interacts with to determine strengths, weaknesses, and areas of improvement. The dean then writes a letter to the chair outlining suggestions for growth and laying out expectations for the next year. In some instances, though, the dean simply has a discussion with the chair at the end of the year and provides verbal feedback. Having something in writing is a good idea because it is formalized, though, so you should consider requesting a feedback letter or email if one is not typically drafted.

Evaluations are important because they are usually (should be, at least!) tied to merit pay raises. However, if the college has half a dozen departments led by department chairs, the standard practice is to simply provide the same percentage pay raise for the year across the board to not upset the dynamics of the system. It is never wise (or true) to tell all the department chairs that they performed the same, but sometimes this is viewed as simply the least controversial option. I know that an HR professional reading this is shuddering because that is definitely not best practice to blindly apply the same pay raise, but ask most deans, and they will tell you that they would rather not get into long, drawn-out tussles over a few thousand dollars of merit pay raise.

A proper evaluation usually has a self-evaluation followed by the actual evaluation with specific, point-valued metrics. Each person must be evaluated by their supervisor carefully with rationale for the points that they provide for each metric. Then, the supervisor must meet with the chair and explain the evaluation of each category that should contain strengths, weaknesses, and expectations for the following year. The supervisor must also give the chair the opportunity to respond to this evaluation. Both the chair and the supervisor must sign these evaluations so it is on record with the university. In practice, this is often difficult to follow, or not followed for various reasons. Nevertheless, if you want to keep contention out of the evaluation process, you should have an impartial evaluation plan in place so you can point to these documents if the need arises, like in the dreaded instance of litigation (which we will discuss in a later chapter).

- **How long is the term?** Is the job term four years? Five years? Or even less? The term of a department chair entirely depends on the university's policies. So, it is best to check this before you embark on this journey because it gives you a timeline for setting expectations and goals. If your offer letter states that you must increase enrollment by X% before four years—there you go. You know your marching orders! You also need to know what happens after the end of the first term. How does reappointment work? Just about every university has its own way of reappointing department chairs, or for that matter, terminating a chair's position either in the middle or at the end of a term. Make sure that you read the faculty handbook carefully and get clarification from the dean.

- **How is your salary structured?** Base pay, summer salary, stipend? What happens to your salary when you are no longer chair? These are very important questions that you should get answered before you sign on the dotted line. Your offer letter should clearly state the salary structure (base pay, stipend, summer salary, incentives, etc.). However, when you are no longer chair, you will revert to a base pay of some sort. Make sure that you understand every facet of this structure. Even if you feel certain that you will move from one administrative position to another and that you will not return to the rank of professor on a 9-month salary—life happens. The university may decide to terminate your position midway through the term of four years, and then you have no choice but to be a professor. This happens in many cases. You simply cannot predict any of these possibilities, so it is always better to be safe than sorry.

- **What kinds of benefits are provided?** It goes without saying that you need to do a thorough job of reviewing health, retirement, and other benefits that are important to you and your family. Look through the Human Resources website and talk to an HR professional on campus. Clarify things like how long it will take to become vested in the retirement system, whether a pension plan exists, and if there is a 403B plan to which you can contribute. Some other important questions to ask include: Does the university offer a matching percentage or dollar amount for retirement accounts or charitable donations? What are the deductibles for health plans? Is there a health savings plan? How about vision, dental? All of these are important questions, and the answers will affect you and your family. If you have children or are planning to grow your family, also ask if there is a reduced tuition waiver plan for family members.

- **Can the dean unilaterally remove you from your job?** You should always be aware of the perils of leadership. Depending on how your department is structured and the policies of the university, the dean may have the final authority to remove you from your position as chair and send you back to the department where you were tenured originally to serve as professor. In some cases, policies in faculty handbooks stipulate that the dean cannot remove a chair without consulting faculty and acquiring a majority vote. Possibilities like this are why it is of utmost importance to be very familiar with the contents of any applicable handbooks. Know the policies so you can advocate for yourself. Typically, a department chair cannot be removed from his position without due cause, but due cause can be a subjective standard, and ultimately you are at the mercy of your administration when a tough situation arises.

I know a department chair who was removed because of gross negligence, inability to handle budgets and students, and violation of many personnel policies. Moreover, she had the habit of constantly going above the dean and talking with the provost and president. I know of another department chair who was simply "not popular" with the faculty. So, the faculty drafted a letter, met with the dean, and, as a majority, communicated that they wanted a different chairperson. The dean concurred and replaced the chair. Most of the time if the chair handles the affairs of the department with care and invests effort in completing their duties, things work reasonably well. They are never perfect, though! If a few contentious faculty members, an incompetent chair, a wavering dean, or a weak provost are part of a university's structure, then trouble may brew quickly.

- **Should I have an umbrella insurance policy?** Umbrella insurance policies are a type of asset protection that can give you peace of mind about the crazy "what ifs?" of life. If you do not have an umbrella policy, this may be a good time to explore the options offered by your personal insurance provider. Sometimes the affairs of the department go wrong very quickly. Faculty members can become disgruntled over a myriad of issues. This is why the department chair needs to have the skills to navigate situations carefully. In most universities, if a faculty member is unhappy with the chair, there are processes in place to address the complaints. The faculty member will file a formal grievance with the dean, and an investigative process will commence.

  Sometimes issues may be related to Diversity, Equity, and Inclusivity, and the appropriate office on campus will also get involved. The department chair, and the faculty, for that matter, can each seek the Office of Legal Counsel at the university to know their rights and responsibilities. Sometimes situations reach resolution with a commonsense approach; discussions and conversations can clear up misunderstandings, and life moves on. However, recently a department chair said to me, *"Gone are the days when I could simply have logical*

*An umbrella policy is a wise safeguard for
unexpected, contentious situations.*

*conversations to solve personnel problems. Everyone wants to lash out
with formal written grievances and avoid discussing issues face to face."*
He may have something here. As I listen to department chairs around
the country, this seems to be a difficult and emerging problem. A
quick look at some of your email inboxes will tell you that conflict
management seminars/workshops are on the rise (all for a price, of
course!). Department chairs should strive to work with faculty to
solve problems amicably within the department. If grievances spill
over to the next level—which means that the faculty member will
seek outside counsel and go through a litigation process—your job as
chair just multiplied. While your university's Office of Legal Council
will help you prepare for these situations, it is wise for you to have an
sumbrella policy, just in case. You have a car, home, life, and health
insurance policies. The umbrella policy will help cover additional lia-
bilities like a lawsuit against you that is not covered by your typical

policies. Paying the monthly fee is well worth the peace of mind that the policy offers. Consider it as a cost of leadership.

- **What happens if a faculty member files a grievance against me?** If you have never heard of or had an encounter with a disgruntled faculty member, consider yourself fortunate. However, it is quite likely that you will experience this as department chair sooner rather than later. Most faculty go about their daily business of teaching, doing research, and serving in various capacities, but they always keep an eye out to see if the department chair is doing his job. If things are going smoothly, then they will mostly leave you alone and only knock on your door when they have a special request. However, if they decide that the chair is not a good advocate for the department or is incompetent or lazy, then the grumbling will start.

  Let's talk about a scenario that may be common in some departments. We will assume that a faculty member is hired from another university, and everything looked normal during the interview process. A few months later, though, the faculty member starts demonstrating confrontational behavior. The faculty member becomes increasingly vocal about nearly everything. He walks into your office and first complains about the lack of office space, and then a few days later about course assignments, and then about lack of communication. You realize that he is becoming an unwelcome fixture in your office, and the complaints keep mounting. You think, *"Wait… did the committee or I miss something major about this person during the interview process, or are these problems real?"* After some soul searching, you figure out that these problems are not really problems; the faculty member is a perennial complainer! Maybe your department always has worked so well with very few issues that you forgot to do due diligence before hiring the faculty member. Or perhaps the HR department in your university missed the mark by not doing a full review of the candidate's background before sending the offer letter. Whatever the case may be, this is now a huge problem which has landed squarely in your lap. Not only does this faculty member come to you in person with complaints, but also he sends you long, rambling emails in which he airs his grievances. To make matters worse, the faculty member begins to level accusations against other faculty members in the department.

In a moment of despair, you start searching the internet to see if this faculty member had similar issues previously. After a few minutes of searching, you arrive at a website that says that this faculty member had raised similar issues at his previous institution and sued(!) the university for discriminatory procedures. Now you realize with a sinking feeling in your stomach that due diligence was not done before hiring this faculty member. What happens now?

The department morale begins to slump as the faculty member peppers his colleagues with criticisms. Other faculty avoid the complainer like the plague, and faculty meetings are contentious. This is the moment when the department chair must exhibit strong leadership, otherwise this one faculty member can cause a department to crumble. You probably know that it is only a matter of time before the faculty member takes the "informal" complaints to a "formal" level. After all, he has a history of doing this elsewhere. As empathetic leaders, we often initially give everyone the benefit of the doubt, hoping that things can be turned around. But be aware that sometimes things take a turn for the worse, despite your best efforts at reconciliation.

The faculty member could move from simply complaining to raising his voice, and if left unchecked, could escalate to yelling and temper tantrums. As chair, you need to be aware of your surroundings and how to deal with such faculty members. First, when he launches into a diatribe, be in the habit of taking notes and having a folder that documents the nature of the complaints, what the faculty member said (as closely as you can follow), and your responses. If it ever gets to a stage where formal grievances and lawsuits are filed, this type of information will be used to build a case.

It's fair to tell the faculty member that he cannot simply wander into your office any time he pleases. Ask them to describe their problems via email, and ask the faculty member to contact your staff assistant to set up a time to discuss these items in an organized manner. Moreover, make sure that your staff assistant is present during these meetings to take thorough notes. After the faculty member leaves your office, write a synopsis of the meeting, the issues, and action items, and send this to the faculty member as an email. This ensures that you are responsive, and no one can blame you later for a lack of attention. I'll emphasize this again—document everything carefully. Never, ever allow the situation to get out of hand. If the faculty member walks into your office and starts screaming, get up from your chair, walk towards the door, and ask them to leave. If the problem persists, call the campus police or security in the building. At this stage, you should not only be documenting these issues but also calling Human Resources and telling them about the incident. Events like these must be documented and reported, otherwise no actionable items exist for the university.

While the case I described may seem extreme, I have heard of situations like this in various manifestations. Strong leadership is needed to handle difficult faculty members. Approaches like attempting to offer some discretionary funds or a new office to appease them will not be long-term solutions. That is a sign of weak leadership. No matter how uncomfortable it might make you feel, tackle the issues head-on. Your faculty and staff are expecting you to lead from the front to address discord when it arises.

Leaving your current university

If you are an internal candidate for the department chair job, you can safely skip this section for now. I do suggest that you eventually read it, though, because you may want to apply for another position elsewhere in a few years and will need to know how confidentiality is handled.

When you become interested in a department chair position at another university, the first question that may cross your mind is, "*What if people in my current department find out about my application?*" If you are currently a department chair and wish to become chair at another university, or if you are a professor wanting to transition into a department chair position, the same principles of confidentiality apply. You may have received a phone call or email encouraging you to fill out an application for an open position, or perhaps a friend or colleague suggested the opportunity to you. Maybe you simply found out about the job through an online posting. Regardless of how you learn about the open chair position, the university should have a standard set of confidentiality measures (but it never hurts to ask). It is not out of line to call the current department chair before you apply to ask questions about the process, especially confidentiality.

You typically do not want your current university to know that you are embarking on this journey, because not everyone understands why you may be thinking of leaving. There are several possible options. You could be upfront and let your current department chair and dean know that you are applying to other places. This approach is taken very rarely because there is no confidentiality required in the process. Depending on your position and influence in the department, it is quite possible that the dean or another administrator may talk to you about "retention incentives" such as increasing your pay and providing desired resources. If you are a valued faculty member, the administrators will make these offers to deter you from even starting an application. I have definitely seen this happen before. However, if you desire to go through the process regardless of any enticements to stay, that is your prerogative.

When you speak with the department chair of the university to which you are considering applying, you ask for details about what kind of confidentiality process they follow. You should be assured by the chair that all interviews are confidential until the point where reference checks need to be made during the offer process. At this point it will be difficult to keep the news confidential. You should be prepared to let your current university know that you are moving to another organization. This is why it is important for the application process to start early and finish early so you are fair to your current university. informing your current university just a week or two before the semester starts that you are leaving is unfair because it is nearly impossible to find a replacement (albeit temporary) to teach the courses that you were supposed to teach. Plus, there are a myriad of other things that need to be accounted for. When you become department chair, you definitely do not want to deal with the aftermath of a faculty member leaving at the last minute!

When should I reveal to my current colleagues that I'm applying to become department chair at another university?

The timing of when you tell people about your aspirations is somewhat up to you. You can opt to share this news early on before you even send off an application, or you can wait until it's practically unavoidable. Be aware that if you list colleagues at your current university as references, then the cat will be out of the bag once they are contacted. It's best to at least prepare your references in advance and inform your current chair (or dean) if you reach this point in the application process.

Let's assume you are offered the chair position at another university and decide to accept their offer—congratulations! What if there were internal candidates who applied but did not get the job? Or what if the current chair served as an interim and is now returning to professorship? These situations are not uncommon, and while they may turn out to be non-issues, you should be prepared to tactfully handle professional relationships with these colleagues in case they harbor grudges.

Let's imagine that the interim chair of the department that you will be running was also an applicant for the department chair position. For whatever reason the university decided to not choose this person for the job and instead selected you as an external candidate. This interim chair is a senior member of the department, a professor with excellent credentials, and she stepped up to take on the leadership role of interim chair while the university conducted a search process. Despite these positive characteristics, the university still decided that you are a more ideal candidate. When you arrive on campus, you will hopefully already be aware that she was interim chair and an applicant to the permanent chair position. Remember that the interim chair is potentially a wonderful resource because she knows all the details of the department processes. She knows the budget model, the scope of resources and facilities, and maybe she even has an excellent rapport with the staff assistants. It's best to start with the assumption that she is a reasonable, gracious person who will lend you support. She could readily provide information, wish you well, and step back into her role as a professor with no issues at all. This ideal outcome does happen sometimes.

Be prepared for alternate outcomes, though. The interim chair could be bitter and disappointed that she was not selected for the job and either overtly or covertly create problems for you. Maybe she relies on her close, professional relationships with department staff to seek inside information about department affairs and your decision-making tendencies, or perhaps she makes divisive comments in private conversations with other faculty, causing factions to take shape in the faculty ranks. She could even try to undermine you at faculty meetings by voicing unnecessary judgmental comments or criticisms. You must take these things in stride and let your credentials, management style, and leadership speak for itself. It's a good idea to have honest conversations with the former interim chair to let her know that her actions are affecting other faculty in the department and your role as chair. It is quite possible that discussions like this could influence her to change her behavior, and after a period, emotions and grudges subside. Also remember that this person has a wealth of information, and it may be a wise move to ask this person to lead an effort for the department such as graduate school recruitment or enacting part of a strategic plan. Inclusive strategies like this can convert an adversary into an ally.

Before you begin the job

Ideally, the selection and interview process of a department chair finishes with plenty of time for you to negotiate and accept the offer. This should leave you with a few months before you begin your new role. Let's assume that you accepted the offer March 1, and your start date is set for June 1. This means that you have three months to prepare. If you were an internal candidate, you would already know the department fairly well, and you will not have to devote attention to dealing with all the details associated with moving to a new city. However, if you are coming from the outside, you will have a much longer to-do list. The negotiation stage of the hiring process is when you should ask questions about any funds available to pay for your travel to and from the new area to look for a home and get familiar with the campus. Whether you are single or have a family, there are many steps involved in moving, and that is why a reasonable amount of time between accepting an offer and starting the job is useful.

Depending on the size of the university, there is probably an office on campus that can help you with relocation details. If you are looking for a house or a temporary place for lodging, the university will put you in touch with real estate experts in the area. You would probably prefer to only move once—from your current home to your new home—but housing markets and negotiation processes can be unpredictable and often drag on for many months. It might be most time-efficient and easiest in the long run to rent for six months to a year in your new city and put your belongings in a storage area. Often, I have heard that this is a better approach. Renting first for a short time allows you to get to know different parts of the city, investigate school options (if you have children), and learn about traffic patterns. How and when you move is a matter of individual choice, but no matter what, moving requires a lot of thought, conversations, and planning.

Apart from dealing with personal matters, the time before you start as a new chair is your one chance to prepare for the job. This means piling on additional work because you are likely still working at your current job, and you have already accepted the job as chair. There will be many loose ends to tie up as you leave your university and current city. You may have a house to sell, possessions to sort through, grants and contracts to transfer, graduate students' futures to discuss, and an office to pack up. Regardless of the challenges that come with moving from one location to another, hopefully you can stay focused on the new adventures and leadership opportunities that await you.

After you have accepted the job, you will have a brief chance to work with the current department chair at your new university. It is definitely a good idea to find the time to travel to your new university once or twice, not just for house-hunting purposes, but to have some critical conversations with the chair to initiate a smooth leadership transition. These are discussions in which you can ask detailed questions about the people and inner workings of the department. Remember that some processes will have already been completed, and you will have no decision-making role in those. For example, the teaching schedules and assignments for faculty will have already been completed for the upcoming fall semester. The annual faculty evaluations will also likely be finished, and if there are any merit pay raises for the upcoming academic year, the current chair will have probably already made her recommendations.

As you make transition plans with the current department chair, be sure to ask for any relevant documents that you think you may need. Here is a non-exhaustive list of items you should consider requesting.

- **Faculty teaching assignments.** Usually, forward-looking departments have a plan of action for the courses that will be offered and taught during five-year periods. This means that the department chair will have a document or spreadsheet of courses planned to be taught every semester at the graduate and undergraduate levels with "penciled in" teaching assignments. Some departments are small enough that a particular faculty member always teaches a certain course. Other departments have the luxury of rotating courses among faculty members. Either way, a preliminary list of courses and teaching assignments should be available.

If no such plan exists, then establishing a course plan should be high on your list of first things to accomplish. Planning in five-year chunks is advantageous because it lets students (especially graduate students) plan their program of study. Granted, there will always be some changes to the plan, but this type of preparation is still necessary. A faculty member may retire, there may not be enough enrollment in a course, or another faculty member may decide to go on a sabbatical. Having a plan in place will allow you to respond more easily to unexpected scenarios and devise solutions.

- **A yearly schedule of events and deadlines.** Print it, highlight it, and tack it up in your office. If no such document exists, don't be shy to ask the previous chair or perhaps a department staff member to do their best to draft one. This document will be your lifeline to being aware of and prepared for major events. No one likes a tardy department chair who constantly misses deadlines.

If you are a teaching and a research-active chair, you will have your hands full with things expected by the dean's office and various other university administrators. One of the best things that you can do is to sit down with your administrative assistant and ask her to build a comprehensive spreadsheet of all known items required by administrators and the expected deadlines (e.g., course schedules for the semester, faculty activity reports, reappointment letters, promotion paperwork, budgets, reports, accreditation requirements, etc.) Then, discuss with her how to accumulate and assemble this information well before the deadlines. If your administrative assistant does not know where to start, suggest going through old emails from administrators' offices sent during the previous academic year.

Part of being an effective chair is to ensure that deadlines are met properly. Your dean is leading multiple departments, and only when she receives information from all departments will she be able to assemble the reports and presentations that she needs to create. If you are always scrambling to provide requested information to the dean, she is bound to get annoyed!

- **Operating budgets for the upcoming and past three years.** It does not matter if you are a small, medium, or large-sized department. The operating budgets are always a point of contention, and there is no one-size-fits all approach to "controlling" the budgets. Remember that your dean manages multiple departments including yours, therefore she has to ensure that financial support for each department is adequate and equitable. For example, the chemistry department may have a large budget because they have several labs that require expensive equipment and supplies, while the mathematics department may be able operate easily on a budget half the size.

  It is always useful to know some details about how money flows from top to bottom in your university. As incoming department chair, you need to know how much money was allocated to your department for the past three years and exactly how it was spent. As department chair, you may want to eventually lobby for more money to create new initiatives, and justifying your plans will be critical to their approval. So, a chair should never ask for more money if he does not understand how funds have historically been spent. If budgets have already been set for the upcoming fiscal year, you may not have the opportunity to ask for more money, but it gives you a good opportunity to study the budget and prepare for the future. Some deans are fond of only using past history for operating budgets as the budget model. (Terrible idea, but it nevertheless happens.) This approach leaves little room for starting new programs and implementing novel ideas. Also, as I mentioned in Chapter 2, this is why you should seek external funding sources for your department. Income that is independent of the university will give you greater flexibility in running your department according to your vision.

- **Access to annual faculty evaluations.** As an incoming chair, you ought to gather some information about the performance of your current faculty. The best place to obtain that material is not from your faculty's CVs and websites but from the faculty activity report (FAR). Each year, faculty members compile a report (usually online) about their teaching, research, and service portfolios, and the chair provides a written assessment with ratings (usually ranging from Excellent to Poor). Therefore, studying the FAR will offer you a clear picture of the strengths and weaknesses of each faculty member. Pay special attention to the sections that allow the faculty to freely express their views or future plans. These are usually the sections in which faculty air their grievances. Remember that the FAR is only a small piece of truly getting to know the faculty. Once you arrive at the university and start your work as department chair, your one-on-one conversations with the faculty and continued relationship building with them is the most important aspect of learning about them both personally and professionally. Depending on the university, you may have to wait until Day 1 of your new job to look at these evaluations—but you can always ask.

- **List of current and potential donors.** If you are inheriting a department that has already cultivated good relationships with donors and there is a solid history of giving to your department, then consider yourself to be among the chosen few. You now have the responsibility to cultivate these relationships after you become chair. If the department has not traditionally received many donations, then you should create initiatives to raise funds—either in conjunction with the Office of Endowment at your university or on your own.

Chapter 2 Summary

In this chapter we...

- **Outlined some advised "initiative" actions you can take prior to submitting an application.** Even the most experienced and prepared applicants can benefit from learning more about academic management at their own university (if that's where they are applying to be chair) or at universities in general. And the best way to learn is through experience! If an opportunity arises for you to get more involved with a process or initiative, raise your hand. If a department event is scheduled, clear your schedule so you can show up. The more actions you take to develop a better understanding of all aspects of how a department operates, then the better your chances will be of impressing a hiring committee.

- **Surveyed the major stages of and documents involved in the department chair application process.** Applying for a department chair position can sometimes feel like a whole other job in and of itself. The time and focus required to research academic leadership practices, thoroughly update your CV, draft an eye-catching cover letter, write a compelling position paper, and respond to all requests for interviews and meetings may be overwhelming at times. So, planning a lot of travel and scheduling major project deadlines during the application and interview timeframe isn't a wise approach. If you're serious about becoming a chair, you should devote 100% effort to all aspects of the application process.

- **Reviewed interviewing best practices.** All impressions matter, but those that are formed in person (or in video calls) are especially enduring. Make professional choices at all times in how you visually present yourself, what you say about yourself and others, and in the questions you pose to your interviewers.

- **Discussed job negotiation tactics.** To make an informed decision about whether to accept a job offer, you will need to collect a lot of information. Ensure that you have clarity about your individual salary, pay schedule, benefits, relocation assistance (if needed), and teaching and research expectations. Ask as many questions as you need to gather relevant details because your decision will affect many people beyond yourself for years to come, and don't hesitate to respectfully advocate for what you think is fair.

Answer the following questions to learn more about how the chapter content applies to you personally.

1. Try to identify three steps you could take to better prepare yourself for an academic leadership position. Set up a brief action plan for pursuing these opportunities—Who should you contact? What will you need? How will you fit these activities into your schedule? What do you hope to gain?

2. If you were writing a cover letter to go with a department chair job application, what would you highlight about yourself? Name three professional characteristics that you feel make you an outstanding candidate, and write a sentence or two about how you embody or demonstrate these characteristics.

3. Imagine that you have reached the interview stage for a department chair position at a research university (maybe you have already been in this situation!). Try answering the following common interview questions that the college dean or another administrator might ask you.

- How would you articulate your vision for the department's growth and development over the next five years?
- How do you plan to promote interdisciplinary collaboration and teamwork within the department and with other departments at the university?
- How do you plan to facilitate and promote research initiatives and growth within the department?
- What strategies will you use to seek out and secure external funding opportunities?
- How do you plan to enhance and maintain diversity among faculty, staff, and students within the department and establish an inclusive environment that values differences?

Chapter 3.

Getting Started as a Department Chair

YOU SHOULD HAVE SEVERAL goals when you are starting as a new department chair. First and foremost, you should strive to fully understand the structure of the department, the faculty, staff and students, and especially the strengths and weaknesses of the department. This will provide a solid foundation on which you can build initiatives. While it is always important to know the needs of the department (and there will be many), you should clearly signal to everyone in the department that building relationships is also a very high priority. Slowly but surely, you should communicate your concrete vision and goals and how your expectations align with these goals. Faculty are usually excited when they see the department chair as a strong supporter of all department members and a leader who always aims to make decisions based on the "collective good" of the department.

Ok... you read my book, applied for the job, were chosen from a competitive pool of applicants, and your first day as department chair has arrived! Since you take "The you factor" chapter of this book very seriously, you got up early, worked out, ate a healthy breakfast, and you have resolved to hydrate well throughout the day. You get to the office early to begin your day on the right foot.

Your first day will likely be packed with meetings like mandatory human resources sessions and "kick off" conversations with the dean and others.

You may only have a few hours to devote to actual work, but make it a priority to be present in your office and visible around your building. Being present and involved will set an example for your faculty and staff and inform them about what type of department chair you intend to be.

Your staff may be just one administrative assistant, or you may have a team consisting of one or more associate chairs, administrative assistants, academic advisers, budget personnel, and others. Whether you are supported by one staff member or many, it is important that you ask your primary administrative assistant (who will be responsible for your calendar) to set up a meeting with the staff early in the day. Some, if not all, of them had the opportunity to meet you during the interview stage and probably provided feedback on their choice of the best candidate. This initial meeting should have a simple purpose; give them an opportunity to share something about themselves and what they enjoy about serving in their position. Your job is to make them feel that this is a team and that you will work hard to support them. They need to have a sense of ownership in what they do, but it goes a long way when you as their leader verbally state that you are there to support them. Set some expectations in that meeting for teamwork, communication, and respect for one another, and set up a schedule for similar meetings in the future. Often it is a lack of communication that begins to tear teams apart. Communication empowers your staff to do their job well. Lack of communication and support will very quickly lead to discontent, low morale, and isolationism. While I advise meeting with the staff on the first day, this is not the day to schedule your first faculty meeting. Instead, you should send the faculty an email when you first arrive at your desk to let everyone know that you are happy to start your journey and that you will be stopping by to see them soon.

Usually, department chairs start their positions in the early summer (June) when the semester has ended and you've had some time to move from your previous university to the current one. This timing works well because university activities are typically less hectic in the summer, and there will be some time to address any issues before the start of the next academic year in August. Not all faculty may be working during the summer because some may be on nine-month contracts with no research obligations, while others may be on official travel, conducting field experiments, or simply hunkering down to write their long overdue research papers!

The next phase of your work as department chair is probably going to be the busiest, and there are many things headed your way. It does not matter whether you start during early summer when the spring semester has ended or during the middle of a semester when classes are already in full swing. Unfortunately, the types of things that will come across your desk have no logical sequence. You will probably find yourself in "triage" mode much of the time as you juggle all sorts of requests and issues. If there is a short lull in activities, don't be fooled, because a deluge will be headed your way soon. A while ago I met a department chair who had just started his job a few weeks prior. He commented, "*Well, things seem to be pretty quiet, and my team and I appear to be handling things well. We even feel we are ahead on most items!*" I guess he spoke too soon, because a few days later he said, "*Things are definitely no longer quiet. My desk is now stacked with piles of things that are demanding my attention.*" I smiled and told him, "*It is indeed feast or famine in this type of job!*"

While you're still in the early days and weeks of starting as department chair, it's a good idea to get a handle on several things so you will be as prepared as possible to run the department smoothly. You can ask your administrative assistant, other staff members, and faculty to help you acquire information about the items below.

1. First, make sure you have access to all important department files. Hopefully most if not all files will be available electronically. Make a plan to read pertinent items daily or weekly.

2. As I mentioned before, ask your administrative assistant to provide a list of various deadlines for the entire academic year. If a calendar of such deadlines is not already available, this needs to be a top priority. A good department chair avoids deadline "surprises" by being aware of them long before they approach. Ad hoc deadlines will still arise, but deadlines for customary items such as when faculty performance evaluations are due to the dean or when reappointment letters must be completed should also be on a calendar that you can quickly assess.

On the same calendar, add reminders in advance of each deadline so that they are on your radar.

3. Compile course assignments for the current and upcoming semesters. This will give you a good survey of courses taught by faculty, lecturers, and adjuncts (part-time faculty). It will be too early to start auditing course loads, but at least you will start gaining a thorough understanding of the traditional course offerings and assignments. However, this is the time to make sure that you have access to the faculty teaching assignments for the last three to five years. If this does not exist, ask your administrative assistant to put together a spreadsheet and place it in an electronic filing system (like Google drive) so you can readily access it. Make sure that you provide an appropriate deadline for this task, because it should be a high priority. This will become your starting point for assigning courses to faculty in the following semesters.

For science department chairs, it is important to allocate sufficient budget funds for purchasing and maintaining lab equipment.

4. You need to know the number of Graduate Teaching Assistants (GTAs) assigned to your department and what courses they typically help with. Find out how they have supported professors and students in previous semesters, and determine the stipend amounts they have traditionally been offered.

5. If your department has a large laboratory component (e.g., chemistry, physics, or biology), then the lab budget, supply purchasing processes, and who oversees the labs are crucial pieces of information. Also, if there is specialized equipment that requires maintenance, it is important to know the costs and related issues with that equipment.

6. Enrollment information—both current and historical—will tell you much about how your department has evolved (or not) over time. If you offer multiple programs and degrees, this is a good time to obtain data about the number of students enrolled in each option. Gather a list of master's and PhD students by name, program, and expected semester of degree completion. Start the process for the current semester and then ask your team to provide student information for the past three to five years. In an efficient university system, there is probably a database that your administrative assistant or someone from your team can access quickly. Make sure that student information is also in the same electronic folder. If you want to be an effective chair, then having good data is your best ally. Also, if you do not know what the current state of affairs looks like, it is next to impossible to develop and implement a strategic plan. Often ineffective department chairs try to make justifications to the dean and higher administration without appropriate data. This can make you look out of touch with your department. As chair, it is imperative that you have all the data regarding your department handy so that you can access it with a few clicks on your computer or smart device.

7. Obtain a list of all department committees and who leads the committees. Now is not the time to delve into details about the actions

and initiatives fostered that the committees oversee. Plan to follow up with these committees a couple of months down the road.

8. Money matters are always important to your faculty staff, so make sure that you acquire data about what salaries and pay raises that faculty have been receiving annually for the last several years.

9. All information regarding the department budget should be at your fingertips. You need to thoroughly study the budget for the current year and ensure that the budgets for the last three to five years are available for review later.

10. As department chair, you should have an accurate understanding of your faculty's research areas. A good place to find out about the research that they are doing is by reading the annual report (sometimes called the faculty activity report) that each faculty member submits yearly. Make sure that these reports are organized and easily available electronically. These reports should provide information on publications, conference presentations, grants and contracts, and other professional activities.

11. Pay attention to your department's website. There's no such thing as a perfect website, and don't be afraid to offer suggestions for improvement to make it more informative and accessible. A welcome message from you and a list of all your faculty with their pictures and contact information is a must. It is also important to include an abbreviated CV for each of your faculty. Organized and functional links to resources, courses, and other information that your students and stakeholders can access is critical. Be sure to prominently feature any newsworthy items such as awards and accolades earned by your students and faculty.

12. Some buildings and campuses have confusing layouts, so having access to floor plans and maps is handy. These documents will also help you visualize who uses which spaces for their offices and labs.

13. Finally, acquire a list of all open cases regarding faculty, students, and staff. If there are grievance cases involving faculty or students, you need to quickly get up to speed on these cases. This means that you may need to pay a visit to the office of legal counsel very soon to be debriefed about your role and responsibilities.

Interacting with your faculty and staff

Building relationships with faculty. Within your first week on the job, you should plan to meet with each of your faculty one-on-one in their office for about 30 minutes. Yes, in *their* office. Whether you have three faculty members or thirty, you must make it a priority to schedule and follow through with these "listening sessions." Take notes on their comments, and ask a few questions about their teaching, research, and service portfolios. Also ask them some open-ended questions about what they think is working well in the department and what needs improvement. Try to keep discussions from getting bogged down in overly negative and contentious issues. If you take good notes during these meetings, then later you can search for common threads among their comments. If a significant number of faculty are all highlighting a certain issue or two, then you need to pay special attention to those factors. It is also important that you compare your notes with the faculty activity reports to make sure that the items outlined by the faculty corroborate their official reports.

Faculty appreciate competent department chairs who consistently advocate for them and the whole department. But beyond the mechanics of the job, they also prefer personable chairs. At any administrative level, it speaks strongly to your leadership style when you walk the corridors of your department to greet faculty in their space rather than being formal all the time. Of course, there is a time and place for formal meetings, but casual office or hallway conversations are oftentimes very illuminating and help build positive rapport. I am sure that if you are a faculty member reading this book, you can point to leaders who you particularly enjoyed working with because they had easygoing, amiable personalities. It may not be your style to be personable, but I strongly encourage you to maximize the use of your social skills, especially if you are new to the university.

I know of one department chair who would casually walk into faculty offices and have brief but meaningful conversations—authentic ones—about both professional and personal life. He was revered in the depart-

> ### What are your natural communication styles?
>
> Successful leaders communicate clearly and frequently with the people in their organizations. Often this communication happens in formal ways through emails and group meetings, but some of the most valuable communication occurs in one-on-one and small group conversations. In these settings, it's important to be aware of both how you tend to interact with others and how others prefer to engage. Do you often find yourself dominating a conversation, sharing your thoughts and opinions while others simply nod and listen? (Many leaders are this way!) Or do you tend to quietly consider ideas and let others steer the conversation? Different situations will require different approaches. Be cognizant of how you naturally participate in dialogues so you can adjust as needed to get to know and work well with your colleagues and staff.

ment because he was seen as genuine, empathetic, caring, and a leader who put people first. The department chair himself may not think of himself as having all those qualities, but his actions and words clearly evoked a positive response from his faculty. Trust me when I give this advice, though: either do this genuinely or not at all. If you are personable for the sake of gaining information or for other self-serving reasons, faculty will quickly sniff it out and lose any trust they have in you.

I am often asked when and how faculty respond the best to department chairs, and I give a pretty simple answer. Faculty must trust that the efforts of their department chair are genuine. Of course, the chair must have excellent credentials with solid communication skills. But the ability to listen, engage others, and yet make difficult decisions for the collective good clearly signals to faculty that they have a leader who is looking out for them. Faculty also need to know and see that you are not only excited to do the job of department chair but also intend to work hard at it. A lazy chair is one who likes to delegate and form committees when he does not want to do the work himself. Writing the first draft of a vision/strategic plan with input from faculty, getting involved in curriculum-related matters, finding ways to raise funds, and coming up with creative ways to recruit and mentor students are all things that department chairs should lead with authority. Once faculty know that you are there to help alleviate some of the administrative burdens on their lives, they will roll up their sleeves quickly to serve the department.

As chair, you should get to know each faculty member at a professional level so you can help them achieve their goals. Developing these relationships takes time because trust must be built carefully. Not every faculty member can be at 100% in teaching, research, and service all the time. Each person has his or her personal strengths and weaknesses. Regardless of their career stage, it is your responsibility to nurture a connection with them, build trust, and encourage them to do their best work.

Take this case, for instance. A department chair who was at least 15 years younger than his senior colleague quickly figured out after a semester or two of being the chair that the senior faculty member had a lot more to offer than just teaching upper-level graduate level courses with a few students. While the senior faculty member was well respected by national and international research communities due to publishing numerous research papers and managing a well-funded research team, he only taught the same graduate-level classes year after year. The department was short-staffed, and the chair always had to hire adjunct faculty to teach an undergraduate course that the senior member could have easily taught. The senior faculty member had an aversion to teaching undergraduates, though. He believed that teaching such courses was time-consuming, and undergraduate students were not ready for the rigor that he expected. He also thought there were too many students per class to teach at the level and in the style that he was used to.

Over one to two semesters, the department chair convinced the senior faculty member to simply try teaching one undergrad class, and if it did not work out, he would never be asked again. It takes a lot of relationship building for a chair to get to this point with a faculty member, but it also takes insight to predict that this faculty member could absolutely love teaching that course and potentially change the lives of several students. Reluctantly, the senior faculty member took on this undergrad class of 30 students. After a few weeks of getting to know the students, he realized that there were some amazing pupils who did outstanding work and really appreciated what he was teaching them. Who doesn't like that? Student evaluations corroborated what he already knew—his teaching "experiment" was a success, and the students advocated for him to teach the course again next semester The senior faculty member then realized that his research program could benefit greatly by providing a pipeline from undergraduate to graduate levels, so he started planning to add undergraduate research opportunities within his team. The senior faculty member never complained again about having to teach an undergraduate course.

After two semesters, the chair stopped by the senior faculty member's office and casually asked if he was ready to give up the undergraduate course to someone else—a new hire in the department. The senior faculty member responded by describing how he sincerely loved to teach that course and could not bear to part with it. The department chair smiled and assured him that he could keep the course as long as he liked.

These are the types of success stories that you can feel good about and recount years later. Turning things around, changing perceptions, building trust, and encouraging faculty to work at a level they never imagined can be the fruits of your labor if you put in the time and effort.

Building relationships with staff. As soon as you begin your job, you also need to set up one-on-one meetings with all staff members to get a sense of their job duties and how things operate. This may not be the time to get a complete list of all the things that each staff member wants to improve, but it is reasonable to ask them to share the top three things that they would like to see evaluated and/or changed. Take good notes, and assure them that you will continue discussions with them soon to learn more about their thoughts and perspectives. Whether you have one staff member (usually an administrative assistant or staff assistant) or have several staff members (a budget manager, several staff assistants, an endowment officer, or assistant/associate chair), this is your team that will help you run the affairs of the department. If your goal is to truly forge a smoothly operating team, the most important thing is to ensure that you are all on the same page about how to work together to accomplish tasks. Here are a few things to keep in mind.

1. **Communication.** Effective communication is absolutely critical for an efficient, successful team. This means that you cannot "forget" to communicate important items or neglect to share information. Here is what one chair stated:

   "I met with the dean every month to give him a quick rundown of my departmental affairs. Sometimes these meetings were short, and other times they lasted nearly an hour. I made sure that I took thorough notes, especially about what the dean asked me to accomplish. One of the first things that I did after the meeting was to call an "all hands" meeting with my staff. Everyone knew approximately when I would be back after my meeting with the dean. Unless there were extenuating circumstances, attendance for my immediate staff was mandatory. In this meeting I shared my notes with the staff, and we drafted a list of action items. This helped ensure that there was no miscommunication."

   This chair's proactive, organized approach to communication was a slam dunk. He kept the timeline for communication among the dean, his staff, and himself as short as possible so ideas and momentum were not lost. This is an approach that I highly encourage you to emulate!

2. **Trust.** You must lead the way in building an atmosphere of trust that allows people to make decisions without being micromanaged. Your team also needs to trust you that if they make mistakes, you will be there to help through the problem and find the appropriate solutions. Trust is not built overnight, of course, so you should commit to con-

sistently telling and demonstrating to your staff that your primary goal is to support them so they can do their best work.

3. **A collegial atmosphere.** Like it or not, for four to five years (or more!) you will spend a lot of time with your staff members, sometimes more than eight hours a day. Therefore, creating a caring, collegial atmosphere will go a long way toward building a positive workplace. One administrator I know said, *"Every other Friday I'd stop by a local bakery and buy a loaf of cinnamon bread or whatever was freshly baked that day. I would take it to the break room, put on a pot of coffee, and invite the staff to spend about 15 to 20 minutes catching up on non-work-related events. This soon became a bi-weekly event that we all enjoyed and looked forward to."*

Not every moment of the workday must focus on work. Getting to know your faculty and staff members on a personal basis is worthwhile in building rapport.

4. **"I got your back" mentality.** Teams work well when each team member knows that everyone is looking out for each other. When a mistake is made, as chair of the department, you need to take care of the issue in private, not call out one of your team members in public. Here's what a staff member had to say, "*We were in a faculty meeting, and one of the faculty members was irritated that some paperwork was not finished quickly enough. I was surprised when my boss, the department chair, said—Well, my staff assistant was absent that day, and that is the reason the paperwork was not done.—I felt like I was being thrown under the bus by my department chair!*" When teams cover well for one another during absences, that's a good sign that the team is working well. However, when a team member basically says, "Well, that's not my responsibility," it shows that they are not willing to be a team player. As chair, you should set an example by demonstrating that you have your staff member's backs, especially when they are clearly doing the best job they can.

Working with your administrative assistant (AA). Your AA will be one of the most important people in your life during your tenure as chair. He or she will serve as the anchor to your team, so you must establish a relationship built on trust. Empower and support your AA properly, and this person will emerge into a lifelong ally and friend. They will go the extra mile to ensure that the department runs smoothly. If you do not support them well to do their job, you are simply buying trouble. Sometimes you will inherit an existing AA who has been in the department for a while. Other times, you will have an opportunity to hire your own. Like the "faculty member types" that I will outline later in this chapter, administrative assistants also tend to have particular profiles and characteristics.

1. **The "9 to 5" AA.** Have you ever met one of these? They pack up their bags well before 5 PM and watch the clock in anticipation of the moment they can escape. Like Cinderella at the stroke of midnight, she vanishes from her office. I have met this type of AA. She won't work a minute more than she must, but she also fulfills her duties. She is consistent, but inflexible in her work schedule. Under

no circumstances should she be disturbed during lunch; she has even posted a warning message on her door about disrupting her "me" time. On one hand, it is important to have boundaries at work, but this level of rigid boundaries means that she will not go an extra inch, let alone an extra mile, to help faculty, students, and other staff. The role of an AA, much like the department chair, is to serve the department by helping to create a positive, smoothly operating work environment. Her influence can set the tone and example for other department members. Therefore, a "9 to 5" AA may not fit the paradigm for your department.

2. **The "royalty" AA.** In a team that has multiple staff assistants, your AA may be the type that clearly wants to be the "king of the hill." Watch out because he will filter every decision you make through that lens. He wants to be the first one to know all the details, purposely avoids sharing information with other staff assistants, can easily develop hurt feelings, and is quick to play the "no one appreciates me" card. As department chair, it is your responsibility to ensure that staff members clearly understand their expected roles and responsibilities. You should frequently reiterate the fact that the entire team—including you—is there to serve the department. To that end, it is unacceptable for any staff member to consider themselves more privileged or important than another.

3. **The "minimalist" AA.** Much like the "do the minimum" FM, this AA sets her bar low. You walk into her office, and you find her reading a book or surfing the web. When you proceed to say that you want something done quickly (copies of a paper for a class that starts in half an hour), she gets up, walks to the copy machine with you, and shows you how to operate it—as though you do not know how to do it yourself! Or better yet, when asked to fill out a form for recruitment, she just sends the form along to you without bothering to work on it herself. She may think that she is simply adept at delegating tasks, but in reality, she shirks her duties. This type of AA hardly gets involved in "trivial tasks" and expects others to com-

plete them instead. Needless to say, she has plenty of free time. Long lunches, unexcused absences, and taking care of personal business during the day are all hallmarks of this AA. When the department chair is out of the office due to travel, she comes and goes from her office as she pleases, sometimes not appearing at all. This type of AA sets a dangerous precedent for other staff members, and you will need to directly address these unprofessional behaviors with her.

4. **The "busybody" AA.** This AA seems to be in everyone's business. While this may be an efficient (or not) AA, he loves being "in the know" about the personal details of everyone's lives. He works hard at accumulating information (gossip) and then freely passes it on to whomever he happens to chat with in the hallway. If you ever wonder how confidential department information makes its way to unintended ears—you've found your leak! This AA will likely be particularly popular with other faculty, staff, and students because he provides a "listening ear," but watch out—it's only a matter of time before his oversharing leads to problems.

5. **The "gold standard" AA.** In just about every part of this book, I have used examples from various department chairs to explain situations. However, here I will use an example from my own experience. I have had the privilege of working with an AA who is truly "gold standard" material. She always arrived early at her desk, setting a positive, energetic tone for the day. I also enjoy getting an early start on the day, but I quickly figured out that the beginning of a working day was something she liked to own—so I opted to start my days a bit later. She made sure that my calendar was managed carefully, shielding me from unnecessary work. She was gracious, kind, and compassionate, but also firm when she needed to be. She did not put up with nonsense. Her office had a steady stream of people in and out every day, but she avoided engaging in long conversations that distracted her from work.

I don't recall talking to her about adopting a service mindset and being a good team member. She naturally had those core values. She would go the extra mile for every student, ensuring that they always had all the necessary paperwork to make their degree path a reality. She was never late in meeting deadlines and made sure I did not miss mine. She had a "sixth sense" about when to interrupt my meetings and when to stay away. Overall, she understood my working rhythms, and I understood hers as well, which made working with her as effortless as possible.

If you are an aspiring department chair or a current department chair, you are probably wondering—can I hire this person? This type of AA is truly worth her weight in gold. She was empowered to make decisions, but she never stepped over the line. She was confident about the difference between what should be a department chair decision and what could be an AA decision. A rare quality indeed! The department prospered much under her guidance. She always remained in the background, but every event that she did—from recruitment to receptions to award ceremonies—was classy and came off without a hitch. I can't imagine what my time as department chair would have been like without her by my side.

Staff management

Interviewing staff candidates. Just like you inherit your faculty, the same could be true for most or all your staff. When you interviewed for the position of department chair, you should have had an opportunity to have a discussion with the AA and perhaps some other staff members. Some staff may have worked for a long time with the previous chairperson and will feel ready to resign or retire soon after you take over as chair. If they were excellent and efficient team players this could be a huge loss, but on the other hand, this gives you an opportunity to interview and hire someone that will fit with your working style and rhythm.

The first few weeks of starting as chair are busy and filled with meetings and appointments. If a staff member does communicate their intent to leave, do not delegate the job of finding their replacement to them or to another staff member. This is especially true for your AA. You must make time to lead the hiring process yourself, because these are individuals with whom you will work very closely. In some universities, human resource specialists have a program where you can hire temporary staff for a period of a few weeks to months to determine if that person may be a good fit for the position. Be sure to ask your dean to provide funding to allow your current staff to train any new members. The dean may protest this as a budgetary issue, but make a convincing argument that even a few hours of training could be immensely helpful to learn critical processes.

If you decide to ask HR to help you find a temporary employee, you need to make sure that you provide the appropriate job description and skill set required. Sometimes you inherit an antiquated system where everything was done through paper stored in physical filing cabinets. While that may have worked for the previous chair, these are outdated procedures, and you should adopt an "online" system with shared drives, electronic forms, and other ways to easily share and review information without generating mounds of paper. Therefore, it is important that you provide a good description of the digital-era skill sets that you expect from your staff.

One department chair's experience may surprise you. "*This was 2014, and I had accepted the job as an administrator. I was amazed at how the whole office was set up. First, there was a receptionist at the front desk who acted as gatekeeper to the office suite. Next, I learned quickly that all calls for the chair came to the AA first, and she transferred the calls to the chair's line. (Really, did he not know how to answer calls directly?) If he was not in the office, the AA left a sticky note for him titled "While you were out"— remember those? She then affixed the notes to his door for anyone to see. All correspondence—reports, forms, important emails—were printed out, and an entire office was dedicated to filing all the paperwork—like an old-fashioned doctor's office. The AA and her student helper spent a good portion of the day copying, stapling, and filing. I knew I was in trouble because I needed all the processes to be done efficiently and electronically. So, my first few weeks were spent modernizing the office. It absolutely had to be done to maintain my sanity.*" This sounds like an extreme case, but office systems are an essential part of work processes. An inefficient system will frustrate you, your staff, and everyone who is expecting a prompt response.

During the interview process for new staff, it is not out of the ordinary to have your current staff member present, even though he or she will be leaving. If you have an assistant or associate chair, they should be part of the interview process as well. While most HR best practices suggest a structured interview that can be rated, ranked, and analyzed later (especially if there are multiple interviewers), you ought to allow enough flexibility to ask some specific questions. Focus on skill sets, and ask specific questions about their organization practices, working rhythms, and ability to multitask and troubleshoot issues. Be sure to provide a clear framework of your expectations for the job in the interview. Good staff members serve as anchors in the department because you cannot stay in your office all the time. You have to attend meetings, travel to conferences, and talk to donors in the community and beyond. Therefore, training your staff appropriately to make necessary decisions will keep processes moving along. If you do not empower your staff to analyze situations and make decisions, then work will stagnate and wait for your return. Therefore, these working relationships are of paramount importance.

With the caveat that every interview should be tailored to the specific department, university, and overall circumstances, here is a list of suggested questions to ask staff position candidates:

- Please explain the working rhythms of your previous job. When did you typically start your day, what types of things did you do, and how did you finish your day?
- Tell us about how you organize multiple tasks with varying deadlines.
- How did you assist and work with your supervisor?
- Discuss how you managed the calendar with deadlines.
- In what conditions do you thrive best?
- In what conditions have you experienced difficulty in your work?
- How do you deal with confidential information?
- Tell us about a time when you had to make a difficult decision at work.
- This job will require working a few Saturdays per year for about two to three hours. Can you handle this type of work?

Letting go of a staff member. Hiring new staff is an involved process, but when you find the appropriate person and you successfully train, mentor, empower them, the whole department can benefit tremendously. Sometimes, though, situations arise when you have to part ways with an employee. Letting go of someone is never easy because there are so many issues at stake. Let's assume that you have an AA who is not performing well. She does not arrive to work at the agreed-upon time; she leaves work for hours at a time with no explanation; and she has repeatedly dropped the ball on some important matters. Making things even more challenging, you hear complaints from your faculty and the students that the AA is rude, impersonal, and unhelpful.

Most academic leaders who I know always seem to give the benefit of the doubt to the AA and try to work through the situation, but at some point, it is time to consider if there are appropriate grounds for termination. I have yet to meet a department chair who is comfortable with terminating a staff member. It surely is a difficult and potentially contentious situation for everyone involved, but the collective good of the department is more important. This is why administering annual fair performance assessments should be a standard part of how your department operates. It is not out of the ordinary to even do a performance evaluation twice a year to ensure that things are working correctly. As long as it is a fair process, the HR department at your university will always agree that more documentation is better, and more frequent assessment and recommendations for corrective action are even better. If you give employees chances to reflect on feedback about their performance, then that may be all they need to alter their behavior and actions. You can either offer or require follow-up meetings with you to go over their evaluations and discuss how they can more successfully support the department in their roles.

Terminating an employee, especially a staff member, will never be simple and painless. Despite the conflict that such a process may cause, remember that an employee's termination may be the best decision for the collective good of the department. Having traveled this road before, I can offer some insight into how a termination process unfolds and some actions you can take to make things as straightforward and respectful as possible.

- First and foremost, schedule a one-on-one meeting with the staff member, and ask your AA to "run interference" for you with any other situations that might require your attention in that time frame. Focus your attention entirely on the employee during your conversation. Make sure that you provide clear and structured feedback on the decision that led to the termination. Aim for the discussion to focus on job-related matters only.
- It is a good idea to invite an impartial third person to the meeting to take notes, because the conversation could become contentious. Often HR may already be involved in this process, so an HR representative may be a good choice to invite to the meeting.
- Be firm, fair, empathetic, and supportive. It is never easy for you or the staff member, but this is a necessary aspect of leadership.
- Provide adequate time for the staff member to transition out of the job. Once the termination decision is made, it is best to avoid delaying the news so that you can give the employee as much time as possible to start looking for a new position.
- Never ask someone else to take care of the termination discussion. That is not fair to the employee and speaks poorly of your management style. I have heard in several instances where a dean or a VP will send their associate to take care of the termination instead of handling the matter themselves. This is disrespectful to the employee and signals weakness or indifference.
- With the help of HR, make sure that all necessary paperwork is completed in an efficient manner. Remember to archive all email threads related to the situation for future reference.

Budget management

Departmental budgets, depending upon the size of the department, are usually small compared to the college or university budgets. The dean controls the department budgets, and she has to make sure that there is a proper method for allocating sufficient operating budgets to each department. Not all departments in a college (I am assuming that several departments make up a college) are of a similar size. For example, in most universities, the highest enrollments in the College of Science are typically in the computer science program. Perhaps only a quarter of that enrollment amount is seen in a mathematics or a specific engineering department in the same College. Therefore, the number of faculty and staff are going to scale proportionally to these enrollment numbers, and the operating budget sizes will also vary.

It is nearly impossible to mention all the things that an operating budget covers. Usually departmental budgets are for printing/mailing costs, computer purchases, supplies for the department, travel costs for recruitment and conferences, furniture, and office upgrades. Some departments are also expected to pay for their own phone bills, and that could add up in a hurry. Departments on shoestring budgets have very little funds for travel and computer purchases, let alone furniture. Depending on the way your university is structured, a portion of the overhead funds (facilities and administration) generated by research and grant expenditures by the faculty could be returned to the department. This could supplement the department operating budget for further growth and expansion. Remember also that you will need to determine if the funds from one year carry over to the next or if you must give the remaining funds back to the college.

Departments that do not seek external grants from funding agencies and organizations generate no overhead funds and will be at a serious disadvantage. If you are a department chair who does not have access to grant funds, you have to be a strong advocate for your department when it comes time to justify your department's needs. Here are some questions to consider:

- What does your budget model look like? A budget model tells you how the department is funded each year. You may not be able to figure out everything in the very first sitting, but the sooner you learn, the better.
- What is your vision for recruitment, and do you have any plans for enhancing recruitment tactics?
- What are your plans for increasing the diversity of your department —faculty, staff, and students? How does this vision dovetail with the budget?
- How will you handle faculty travel to conferences?
- How about professional development opportunities for everyone in your department? Can your budget handle requests for paid webinars, tutorials, or certifications?
- Are you expected to fund graduate teaching assistants from your budget?
- Who pays the salaries of part-time/adjunct faculty?
- Who maintains the operating budget for major instruments and equipment?
- Is it possible to hire students to support department staff?

It is absolutely important that you get to know the budget thoroughly soon after you start your responsibilities as department chair. You have to balance the needs and wants of the department with the budget itself. If you are entering into your position when the department budget has already been set for the academic year, there is very little you can do—but learn, monitor, and understand the budgetary needs and requirements. However, very soon you will need to prepare for the next budget cycle. Proactively ask your dean when budgets will be discussed and requested for the next year. Usually there is a budget template for making your requests and justifications. If there is no template, then draft your own based on what you have learned so far. Your dean will appreciate your efforts at organization, and it can always be adjusted if needed. A short list of typical budget requests includes:

- Operating expenses (copying, mailing)
- Faculty and student travel to conferences
- Recruitment materials to distribute at major conferences
- Open houses for recruitment
- Professional development for faculty and staff
- Furniture
- Computers for faculty and labs
- Classroom upgrades

Keeping your faculty "in the loop" about budget information should be a priority. At least once a semester it is beneficial for the faculty to be presented with a clear and simple breakdown of budgetary items. You

Nobody likes being left in the dark when it comes to financial matters in which they have a stake. You shouldn't feel like you need to share all the fine print about your department's budget with your faculty. However, you should get a sense of what updates they are most interested in receiving. Create a simple slide template for sharing that information with them on a regular basis, and make the slides openly accessible for further review.

should include items like how much money the college provided to the department, the amount of funds donated or awarded from external sources, and the major expenditures above a certain dollar amount. A transparent budgetary system will dispel misinformation and assure your faculty that department funds are being handled judiciously. Some chairs worry that if they allow faculty to view budget details then they will start clamoring for more funds or make hypocritical comments about how the money is being managed. However, this is a myopic view because for a department to feel cohesive, faculty members need to have some knowledge of how the budget is being handled and what the financial vision is for the department. Sharing budget information is a valuable way of demonstrating accountability, and being accountable is a key characteristic of successful department chairs.

One faculty member said, *"I hardly know what's going on with the department's budget. When I ask the department chair, he is rather vague and does not provide any details. I'm not sure what he is worried about; after all, this is not his personal money. How difficult is it to share the "big picture" of what the budget looks like and what the spending breakdown might be for a year?"* These are legitimate questions that a department chair can quickly put to rest by providing the necessary information to the faculty.

Why a mentor is a must

Reading books on academic administration is highly recommended. Even if parts of a book don't apply to your particular situation, you are bound to gather several good tips and spark a few new ideas. It's equally valuable to seek out training through conferences and workshops. Your university may even have deep enough pockets to hire consultants to periodically lead customized training seminars for department chairs. However, there is no substitute for one-on-one mentorship. Ideally, you should request mentorship from a former chair of your department. He or she will have the most background knowledge and the best ability to understand the specific situations that you will encounter. Therefore, the advice they offer will be uniquely valuable. This is especially important if you are new to the job of academic administration and if you are considered an early career department chair.

Having a mentor who is a positive role model allows you to emulate some of their best practices. In my own professional career, I have used this role modeling technique to develop characteristics and qualities based on the behavior, values, and work ethic of my mentor. Oftentimes my mentor has provided valuable personal connection and emotional support.

Some department chairs do not seek out a mentor because they think that it is a sign of weakness to ask someone else questions about how to do their job. What a limiting and arrogant way to think! Good mentors welcome questions, and they think very highly of mentees who are humble enough to ask for guidance and feedback. Avoiding seeking suggestions or constructive criticism from a mentor can affect your job performance and trickle down to impact the faculty, staff, and students. Here are a few pieces of practical advice for seeking mentorship and maximizing the benefits of this relationship.

- Whether you establish a mentor-mentee relationship over lunch or coffee or over the telephone—do it! Do not procrastinate in finding a mentor. In fact, I suggest that you find a mentor even before you start your job as department chair. Your best intentions to "get around to it" will be difficult to fulfill once you step into the role of chair.

Advice from a mentor can sometimes be just the thing you need.

- Find a mentor who has experience as an academic administrator. Sometimes this could be someone from within your department or university, but you may need to consider external options as well. You can even establish relationships with multiple mentors! Each one will have a different perspective on matters which could be very helpful at times.
- It is your responsibility to set up meeting and discussion times with your mentor. Come prepared to your meetings with an informal agenda of items you would like to discuss; being organized will make your discussions more meaningful and useful. Make sure that you frequently ask for your mentor's advice about how to grow as a department chair.

- Ask your mentor for book recommendations. If you are interested in specific aspects of being a department chair or in "big picture" ideas, let them know so they can steer you in the right direction. Even if it's difficult to find the time, make sure that you follow through with your reading assignments!
- Ask your mentor to keep all your discussions confidential. When hashing through difficult issues regarding personnel, avoid using specific names of faculty or students.
- Ask your mentor to hold you accountable for the goals and plans that you establish for your department. Allow them to ask you difficult, pointed questions about your progress.
- Finally, draw from the experiences and best practices of your mentor to develop your own style of leadership.

Faculty member profiles

Unless you are a professional or college coach in a major organization, you cannot put together your own team. You simply inherit faculty, staff, and the rest of your "team" when you become a department chair. Some of these faculty are working towards tenure, and others are already tenured. Those who are tenured tend to feel they should have a stronger voice in just about everything in the department. But those who are still trying to achieve tenure may try hard to capture your attention to "make their mark." One thing is for certain: sometimes you will feel like your department is less of a team and more a haphazard group of unique personalities.

A good friend of mine who has been department chair for nearly a decade (too long, my friend!) often tells me that he feels like he is herding cats every day. I smile because I know exactly what he means. If you are a sitcom writer for a TV show, you get to design the cast of characters—

Much like cats, faculty members are not easy to herd.

the smart one, the attractive one, the elderly statesman, the lazy one, the funny one, the drama king (or queen), etc., but with faculty, you must work with the characters you are given. Even as I am writing this, I feel that this section is what a lot of folks are really going to like about this book. (Everyone likes to talk about a particular chapter titled "Managing your advisor" in my first book, *Navigating Graduate School and Beyond*, even though there are other equally beneficial chapters in that book, if I may say so myself).

Below you will find ten possible faculty member (FM) profiles. Most people are a mixture of two or more of these sets of characteristics, so don't assume these profiles apply exclusively to a single person. You'll probably identify some of your faculty in these profiles, or better yet, you may even find yourself!

1. **The "by the book" FM.** In every email or meeting at a faculty meeting, this person always makes an opening with, "*Well, according to the faculty handbook, we should be…*" They are superfans of quorums and addendums and Robert's Rules of Order. They are fond of drafting lengthy emails and are a little too proud of their exceptional attention to detail. You can count on them to take charge of editing tasks, wielding a red pen (or turning on "track changes" these days) with relish. This is the type of faculty member that you need on your curriculum committee and on the team that helps with accreditation. But beware, their meticulousness means that every process they become involved with will require some extra time to reach completion. However, the finished product will be fantastic!

2. **The "always late" FM.** This is a faculty member that could irritate you quite a bit. They are never on time for anything, ever. Ask them to turn in an annual performance assessment report, and they will completely forget about it five minutes later. Your unanswered emails will languish in their overstuffed inbox, and when you stop by their office, they will earnestly promise to deliver whatever you require by the end of the day. Despite their desire to do better, something will always get in the way and be the "excuse." If they ask to serve on a

committee that requires a report, as department chair, you'll need to have a serious conversation with them about their past delinquencies and what will be required if they are selected to be a committee member. This FM can be frustrating to deal with because you simply can't make someone perform their duties in a timely, professional manner.

3. **The "do the minimum" FM.** This faculty member is probably a tenured full professor who has been there, done that, and now feels she has earned the right to invest minimal effort in most departmental activities. Very few universities have post-tenure reviews, so there are no "real" performance evaluation processes to bring this faculty member in line. Besides barely lifting a finger to help with initiatives and committees, she asks to teach the fewest allowable number of classes, and only on certain days and in certain rooms. Because of her seniority, she thinks her special requests should be prioritized. She readily signs up for easy service obligations, as long as they fall on her teaching days.

   Her daily schedule is also minimalist: drive to work, occupy her office for an hour or less, teach a class, then leave for the day. You hardly ever see her in the office other than the obligatory few minutes before class. To make matters worse, she mostly "teaches" through pre-recorded video lectures, and she fosters very few interactions with her students. Most of her students earn good grades, therefore she typically receives great student evaluation scores at the end of the semester. Plus, you hear from students that the faculty member always provides pizza and other food during the semester.

   This faculty member does no research and has probably not written a peer-reviewed paper or presented at a conference in years. She really doesn't care about annual merit pay raises because she already makes enough money to cruise along. When pushed to do more, this faculty member could even seek sympathy by blaming constraints on a sick spouse or relative (whether true or not). She may even dream up personal ailments and blame them for causing limitations. Be aware of such faculty because they are capable of creating excuses to work less.

4. **The "leave me alone" FM.** Often sliding into a seat at the back of the room (just a minute or two before the "always late" FM), this faculty member reluctantly comes to faculty and committee meetings. He could be a successful teacher and a good researcher, but he wants very little to do with the affairs of the department. He responds to emails simply and promptly, but he has very few suggestions or insights to offer. You get the sense that he is simply biding time for a better job in a better place. Much of his professional and personal life is shrouded in mystery, and he is downright allergic to social events with other department members. It does not matter if you try to engage this faculty member and invite him to be more involved; he simply desires to be left alone.

5. **The "anti-research" FM.** Most if not all departments that I am aware of require three core components of a faculty member's role in the department and the university: teaching, research (or creative achievements, in some cases), and department/university service. As chair, you may inherit a faculty member who, for whatever reason, has lost the appetite for doing research. Many causes could be at the root of this issue, but lack of funding is a common one. The faculty member may have been successful at one point, but along the way she stopped winning major research grants. She has found it too difficult to support students and do all the work required to seek new funding. Often departments pay little attention to faculty members who are successful in writing and winning grants, and when the grant well dries up, the departments don't notice the problem. If this occurs, the faculty member will likely become withdrawn and disillusioned. Depending on the stage of her career and fundamental interest in her field, she may choose to let her research endeavors wither entirely.

   You are lucky if this faculty member readily admits that her research career is over and seeks to contribute to the department in other ways, like teaching more courses. Most often as chair you have to initiate some difficult conversations with her to get her to this point of acknowledgment and convince her that teaching more courses is fair compensation. Why so? You probably have other faculty in the department who are constantly monitoring workloads for the department. They will not be happy if research-unproductive faculty teach the same number of courses as research-productive faculty.

6. **The "I'm back!" FM.** This situation applies to a faculty member who returns to the department as a professor after serving in an administrative role such as chair or dean. He could be a blessing in disguise or a downright curse. Here is what one department chair said who called me frantically to ask for some advice.

"I just started as department chair a few months ago, and I realized that a senior member of the faculty has returned to the ranks of professor after serving as dean. He is making life difficult for me because he has been here for a very long time, and he is constantly talking to other faculty in the department and forming alliances. He also stops by my office to give me unsolicited advice on how to handle various departmental matters. Plus, he is making it difficult for me to assign courses and outline my expectations for him in his new role as professor."

This situation created an ongoing headache for the chair. However, if you are lucky, the former administrator could quietly slip back into the department and be an excellent team player and mentor to you personally. He may be willing to have private conversations with you to share his wisdom and advice. This faculty member is now worth his weight in gold. He is ready to teach, do research, and help the department—as if he never left the role of professor. This is the ideal situation, but in reality, most of these types of FMs will need some time to adjust back to being a professor. Do your best to make this former administrator your ally. As a department chair, if you do not rely on his expertise when you encounter tough situations—it is your loss.

7. **The "gold standard" FM.** Count yourself lucky if you have one (or more!) of these FMs in your ranks. This faculty member is a rockstar teacher with legions of student fans. Her research is top-notch, and it seems like grants practically fall in her lap. She never asks for extra

departmental resources and shares her own space and equipment willingly. She is always prompt and professional, and when asked to serve, she happily pitches in to do her fair share. Students, staff, faculty, and administrators heap praises on this faculty member. She is truly the gold standard and positive trendsetter for your department. If a genie granted you three wishes, your first wish would be for more faculty like her.

*Having many "gold standard" faculty members
is every department chair's wish.*

Make sure that you treat this faculty member properly. As chair, you need to make sure that she is paid well, always respected, offered resources even when she doesn't ask for them. It is quite possible that everyone wants this faculty member to ultimately become an administrator at the university because they admire and trust her. However, resist the temptation to urge her to begin submitting applications for administrative positions too quickly, unless that is clearly what she desires. Prolific producers with the "right stuff" in terms of personality and aspirations are often snatched up by other universities with better pay and resources. These universities are always on the lookout for superstars to boost their programs.

8. **The "never enough" FM.** Oh yes, the probability of you inheriting one of these types of FMs is very high. It does not matter what the circumstances are—this faculty member wants more. He wants more office space, more lab space, better furniture for his office, more funds to hire students, more resources for building and buying equipment to do research, more discretionary money… it never ends. On top of that, he also wants fewer departmental responsibilities and a light teaching load. Often this person also likes to hold you captive in long conversations, extolling the virtues of their amazing research (to lobby for more money and resources). Sometimes they even go as far as telling you how you need to pressure the administration for more funding and facilities. He will never be satisfied with what is already available to him, and you will never hear the end of his requests.

9. **The "rebel" FM.** For your own sanity, I really hope that you do not have one of these FMs. Rebels can create lots of problems, and it takes an entire team to manage such a person. This faculty member often feels that she is entitled to just about everything. She shirks basic practices like filling out paperwork for travel and reimbursements. She treats the department staff assistant like her personal assistant, expecting him to do tasks for her that are beyond his typical duties. She exceeds the limits on allowable expenses for research, travel, and purchases, and it doesn't appear to bother her. Her tactic is to keep doing what she likes until she is directly told to change her behavior.

Yes, this type of faculty member does exist, and it takes a lot of effort to keep them in line because they believe policies and protocols simply do not apply to them. She chooses her own "best practices" and doesn't care what kind of chaos ensues. I had a department chair tell me one time that one of his faculty members did not want to follow established radiation safety protocols in his lab and decided to handle dangerous material outside of the established procedures. This action was dangerous for all the personnel in the lab and the inhabitants of that building. But a rebel FM does not care and probably will show little remorse when reprimanded. Be sure to document all notable issues to keep a thorough record in case it is needed for reference in the future.

10. **The "problem" FM.** I saved the best for last! If the "rebel" FM takes up time and causes headaches, the "problem" FM that we are talking about here will totally drain your mental and emotional resources. Actually, that is the intent of this faculty member; they will build up the pressure as a function of time. It may start very benignly with small requests for more office space or additional funds for graduate students. If you ignore them—which is the wrong thing to do—they will ratchet the pressure up by telling anyone who will listen that you are not treating them properly. Give it some time, and he will exert more pressure by saying that he feels discriminated against. The time-line from the initial, simple requests to damaging accusations can be terribly short, so if you sense trouble brewing, it's best to address it directly and as soon as possible.

I do not want to send the wrong message here. Sometimes department chairs can be inept or biased (knowingly or unknowingly), in which case a faculty member may voice legitimate complaints. This is why proper DEI training is paramount. If it is a real issue, then it absolutely should be addressed, and HR may need to be involved. Whether or not the accusations are valid, I often find that a collegial, smoothly operating department can be thrown into turmoil by one faculty member who views everything through the lens of discrimination. Strong leadership is a necessity in these situations. Weaker department chairs may try to appease this faculty member by simply lobbing resources at him and hoping for the best. However, just wishing that he will go away and not raise these issues again is a passive approach that will only lead to more conflict down the road. Their lens needs adjusting if these problems are going to ever dissipate.

If they are unwilling to have a productive discussion that leads to better understanding and change, then I suggest that you begin taking extra care in documenting how you handle departmental matters. Cases that involve DEI issues are not easy and will involve many offices on campus. If the disgruntled faculty member decides to formally file a case of discrimination against you as chair, then it will take inordinate amounts of time away from all your other responsibilities. Universities handle such situations in many ways, but all of them are expected to investigate the grievances thoroughly. Committees will be formed on campus, and you and selected faculty and staff will be interviewed to ascertain the culture of the department and details about the case itself. During these interviews, stay focused on the facts and not emotions and unnecessary information. Be forthright, but leave personal attacks out of the discussion. If you are a department chair who follows official processes and who deals with faculty in a fair, respectful, and equitable way, you have nothing to worry about. Your faculty will corroborate this, and so will your staff. Be sure to consult Chapter 7 for a more in-depth discussion of how to handle contentious situations tactfully and effectively with your faculty members.

Chapter 3 Summary and Questions

In this chapter we…

- **Discussed how to prepare for your first days and weeks as a department chair.** Transitioning into a new professional role is always at least a bit daunting and confusing, and stepping into a leadership position can feel even more overwhelming. In truth, no one should expect you to fix all the problems and meet all the deadlines right off the bat. The best things you can do to prepare for your new job are to thoroughly review all relevant policy manuals and documents (and ask questions as needed!), ensure that you have access to important files and communication tools, and make an effort to get to know the people (e.g., your administrative assistant, staff, faculty) on whom you will rely for support as you get up to speed.

- **Considered the importance of building relationships with your faculty and staff.** The relationships that you build with your employees and colleagues are like the nutrients needed to create rich, productive soil. If you invest your time and attention in fostering these relationships, you will be primed to cultivate initiatives that garner authentic buy-in. Remember that the best way to understand the types of support that your department members need is by nurturing personal connections with them so that they feel comfortable communicating with you and advocating for themselves.

- **Shared strategies for managing staff and budgets.** If you have never been in a leadership role in which you were required to hire and terminate employees, then be sure to review this section. Also reach out to the human resources department at your university for specific advice when any potentially contentious situations arise. For budget management, there is certainly no one-size-fits-all approach because each department's circumstances are unique. Make it a priority to closely examine previous annual budgets so that you can determine what kinds of budget management adjustments might be most beneficial and reasonable.

- **Described some of the faculty members "types" that you will likely encounter.** The list presented at the end of this chapter is by no means comprehensive, but it is a fairly good representation of the most common professional traits that you will see exemplified in many of your faculty members. The key is to make space for all types of people in your organization so they feel valued, heard, and respected.

Answer the following questions to learn more about how the chapter content applies to you personally.

1. Imagine that you are beginning your new job as department chair. What would be your top 10 priorities in your first week on the job? List these activities/tasks/goals, and estimate how much time you think each would require.

2. Everyone has their own natural communication styles—what are yours? One way of assessing your communication style is through a DiSC profile. DiSC stands for four primary personality profiles: (D)ominance, (i)influence, (S)teadiness, and (C)onscientiousness. Each personality type has unique communication tendencies. Using DiSC assessments has been a common practice in corporate environments for many years, and the results help people better understand themselves and how to interact effectively with others

in a workplace (but remember that these assessments are not necessarily "conclusive" and should just provide food for thought).

There are many free DiSC assessments online with information about how to interpret your results and the impact they have on how you communicate. Find and take a couple of these DiSC assessments, review your results, and write a few sentences about how these results inform your approach to leadership.

3. Having at least one thoughtful, reliable mentor is a "must" for first-time department chairs. Who has mentored you in the past or currently mentors you now? How often do you communicate with them and in what ways? In what ways have mentors supported you in your professional work and decision making? If you do not currently have a mentor, make a list of potential people you could contact to begin developing a mentor/mentee relationship.

Chapter 4.

Managing Processes and Meetings

A SIZABLE PART OF YOUR JOB as department chair is navigating processes and conducting meetings. Processes are always formal and must be executed carefully, but meetings can be either formal or informal. As a professor working in a department, you probably never paid much attention to processes at the department, college, or university levels. Most professors tend to focus on their research and students and only take notice of certain processes when they must be directly involved. A department chair doesn't have the luxury of burying her head in the sand about processes, though. When you have questions, you cannot simply email the dean or his staff assistant to get answers—you need to understand for yourself how things work.

Therefore, familiarizing yourself with the faculty handbook, process manual or whatever your university calls it is key. It is not only important that you know about all the steps of critical processes, but you must also mentor (or teach) your administrative assistant. As one faculty member put it, "*My department chair hardly knows anything about processes. He just asks the staff assistant to find out details from wherever she likes, and often-times she ends up passing along outdated or incorrect information.*" It's not difficult to predict the frustrating consequences that will emerge from this pattern of behavior. Being clear, consistent, and correct in following policies is an essential aspect of your leadership role. It keeps everyone out of trouble. I often advise department chairs to maintain a list of frequently asked questions that come from faculty and students and to diligently compile a list of answers in an easily accessible document. I also suggest they go a step further and place these FAQs and responses on the department website or shared drive so everyone can access them when the need arises.

Often the best way of facilitating policy adherence is through meetings…. meetings, meetings, and more meetings. As a professor, you may have secretly or openly shared your distaste for meetings. However, a department chair must grin and bear it, because meetings will be a standard part of your daily schedule. Meetings are here to stay, and how you conduct them and navigate them is important.

There are some meetings that you have very little control over, such as those with your dean or upper administration. Take good notes, and keep your staff and faculty informed about these meetings. Other meetings you will be able to control—your faculty meetings, for instance. It is your responsibility to schedule them regularly, create helpful agendas, ensure that someone records minutes, and follow proper voting procedures. (I will discuss this in detail later in this chapter.) While formal departmental meetings are necessary and useful, much can also be accomplished in informal meetings with faculty. Of course, there are many other meetings—with students, stakeholders, parents, other administrators, other department chairs, and more. Managing your time carefully to accommodate all these meetings takes skill, practice, and diligence. Finally, get ready for those faculty members who wander into your office and want to "just chat" for a long time. My advice is to develop a few ways of tactfully excusing yourself if these impromptu conversations begin to infringe on your departmental responsibilities.

Mastering the working rhythms of an academic year

Let's assume it has been about a year since you started as the department chair, and as they say, the honeymoon is long over. You should now have a clear sense of all the things that are expected of you in an academic year cycle. While it may seem that you never have enough time to accomplish big tasks like drafting a strategic plan, you should have a good idea of how the academic calendar year flows. Hopefully, you have followed my advice to set up a calendar with deadlines that you and your AA share, so you are fully aware of all the items that are due on a customary basis.

If you've made it to the position of department chair, then you most certainly know a thing or two about the standard events and cycles that occur at universities. But do you really have a good handle on WHOLE scope of events and responsibilities that occupy space on a chair's calendar? Try jotting down a list of prominent, annual events and deadlines that you can recall from a typical academic year, then share your list with a department chair (if possible). What important things did you forget to include or not realize would require a chair's time and attention?

The university has deadlines for certain things, such as when promotion dossiers are due and when courses must be submitted to the registrar for scheduling.

Of course, you will continue to fine tune your schedule for research, travel, self-care, and vacations. The earlier you get a handle on the academic year (AY) calendar, the better off you will be and the more confident you will feel. Proactive department chairs manage their calendars well enough that they consistently find time to focus on "big picture" tasks and projects.

If you are struggling with the AY calendar and time management, then try some of these tactics:

- Go back to basics and do something that I recommend to early career faculty: take stock of what occupies your time on an hour-by-hour basis over a two-week period. Identify what drains your time in this two-week calendar assessment so that you can plan to alter your work patterns to a flow that is more effective and sustainable.
- Carefully assess if some of your work could be delegated to others or if you are managing tasks that really should be in someone else's purview. This should be a careful assessment and not just a way to pass off work that you're not interested in doing.
- Examine how your appointments are scheduled and how well your approach is working. Are your appointments stacked back-to-back causing you to be late to meetings and neglect other work? Do you often miss appointments? Do you find that your meetings tend to run too long?
- With the help of your AA, assess how many times you did not deliver necessary documents to the next level because you did not manage your AY calendar well. This type of assessment will help you adjust your working rhythm in a deliberate manner. It is quite possible that you need to change internal deadlines to give yourself more time to collect and organize information. So, if an external deadline is April 15 and your internal deadline was set for April 10, you may need to move it back a few more days. This type of iterative work to refine your deadlines is going to be important.

- When working with faculty, remember that there are always going to be some who turn in their paperwork late. Cleverly scheduling internal deadlines will ensure timely delivery of documents to the next level.

Remember that only when you master the AY calendar will you find the time you need for your own research and other personal endeavors.

Email, calendar, and digital workflow management

Managing your email. As department chair, if you do not manage your emails well, you are bound to feel like your life is in chaos. When you were a professor and not yet an administrator, if you chose to ignore an email or attend to it later, this probably caused no major issues because no one else up the chain or your team were affected. You won't be afforded this luxury as department chair. If you do not address many things very quickly, the proverbial wagon will soon come to a screeching halt. For instance, if you are part of the approval process to purchase a projector for a classroom and you don't promptly sign the approval and purchase order forms in your inbox, your staff cannot process the paperwork to the next level. The purchase of that projector could be delayed, leading to some disgruntled faculty, staff, and students.

Here's what I suggest, whether you come from another university or you are simply moving up from professor to department chair. In either

Separate email accounts are a handy way to keep messages organized.

case it is a good idea to separate department chair emails from personal email. Every university gives you a personal email account when you start your job—let's say sue.smith@gmail.com. This is where all emails regarding your pay and university business will be directed. This is probably the email address that you will list on proposals and papers that you write. I strongly suggest that you ask for another email address to be created—just for the job of a department chair—such as dept-chair@gmail.com. You can then ask your AA to make sure that all emails related to department chair activities are sent to this email address.

This now separates your correspondence into at least two compartments and provides a way to monitor and respond to emails from two separate accounts, so you do not miss important messages. Plus, when you leave the department chair job, you can simply hand over the username and password to the next department chair so they will have a complete history of the proceedings over your tenure as department chair. Some department chairs are uneasy about operating with this level of transparency, but it's ultimately a smart move. Here's a practical tip: try using two different email clients (e.g., Outlook and Gmail) to manage your "two lives." Just make sure that you can easily access both from a mobile device when you're on the go.

Knowing how to organize your email inbox can also be a powerful skill. Take some time to figure out how to use labels and other features so you can develop a system to prioritize certain types of emails and make sure they don't become buried under less critical messages. Identifying which emails to answer quickly and clear your inbox versus which ones to delegate and place reminders on is going to be key. While it is nearly impossible to check and answer emails every minute—although I have seen some administrators hit the refresh button that frequently—you will need a method for answering emails. No one-size-fits-all approach is going to work for everyone, so you must develop your own. It will take some practice to figure out which emails can wait, and which ones cannot. An email from the dean requesting immediate information or attention obviously needs a speedy reply. If an important purchase needs your review and approval and you are part of a long chain of people in the approval queue, then tend to it quickly so you are not the bottleneck. If an email contains a request or question that can wait, be sure to notify your AA to keep it "on your radar" by reminding you to tend to it at a later date.

Keeping your AA informed of all important emails is critical so she can help keep you on top of things. This is something that you should explain to your AA at the beginning of your working relationship. Ask for her input in structuring a communication plan between the two of you that works well for you both. An informed AA is a first step towards empowering an AA. This means they are aware of virtually all things going on except for any confidential matters.

Managing your calendar. A well-managed calendar is frequently a hallmark of an effective department chair. You may be quite good at managing your current calendar as a professor with a strong teaching, research, and service portfolio. If you already are an administrator and moving to a new university to become the department chair, you probably have a working system in place. For now, I'm going to assume that this is the first time you are going to work with a staff assistant who is going to help schedule appointments, events, etc. I strongly recommend working closely with your AA to manage the calendar instead of simply delegating this task. Before I give you the reasons why I personally take this approach, here are some practical ways to do this.

- While there are many options and software for managing a calendar, I will pick Google calendar as an example. It is better that you own the calendar and give your AA privileges to enter calendar items. This way you can synchronize other calendars yourself like a personal calendar that you share with your family and a research calendar that you share with your research team.
- Expecting your AA to manage all the nuances of your personal calendar is unrealistic. This is the reason why you need to have access to your own calendar and mark items that the AA can and cannot see.
- I usually look ahead into the semester and mark on the calendar when I am planning to take my vacation. Once that is entered, the AA can see this calendar item and will not schedule meetings in this timeframe.

- Rather than "telling" the AA when you are not available for meetings, you can simply go into the calendar and mark events and time blocks with the phrase "Away from Office." It is not necessary that you explicitly state that you are playing golf or exercising or having lunch with your child. The phrase should simply communicate that you are unavailable. You can also use this tactic to designate time for research on your calendar.

- After you enter the items described above, your AA can then use the calendar to insert meetings. You will need to work with your AA to explain your working rhythms, and it will take some time to get things running smoothly. Cramming meetings every 30 minutes is never a good idea because if one meeting runs late, then you end up with a domino effect on any following meetings. People feel slighted very quickly if they are kept waiting.

  One chair said, "*I know that meetings are a big part of a chair's life. It took a while, but my AA and I arrived at a good working arrangement where two days a week were 'meeting heavy' days. There was almost nothing else I could accomplish in those days except meet with people and possibly provide debriefs. My AA made sure that the other three days were 'meeting light' so I could work on other aspects of being department chair. Of course, both of us understood that 'meeting light' does not mean no meetings at all. There is always the odd fire that needs to be put out or an urgent personnel meeting, or occasionally the dean wants to see me immediately. Regardless, it was a system that we worked through, and a working rhythm was established. Most importantly, I stopped complaining that my days were too fragmented to get anything useful done. I knew that on the "meetings days" I would not accomplish much, but the meetings actually gave me time to think through items for the other three days.*"

- Work with your AA to set up reminders. If you're having a meeting in your office, maybe a reminder sent 15 minutes prior is enough, but if it's a meeting across campus that requires you to fight for a parking space, you need to have a reasonable amount of time to show up for your meeting on time. An AA shared with me, "*I finally thought I had a good working arrangement regarding calendar items with my boss, and she was extremely busy every day. Even though she carried a smartphone and a tablet, she insisted that I print out her calendar for the day—every day—and place it on her desk before she arrived. I never saw the point of it, but if that is what she wanted, that is what was done."* Again, there are many ways to approach calendar management with your AA, but communication and maybe some trial and error are key to developing a trustworthy system.

I hope the reasons for co-managing your calendar with your AA is a bit clearer after reading these tips. Using this approach, you do not have to wait to verbally tell your AA all the things that you plan on doing such as taking a vacation or carving out some "deep work" time in your schedule. However, be careful not to over-manage your calendar on a day-to-day basis, because you may not know about the "holds" that your AA is placing for potential meetings that involve multiple people.

Automating your digital workflow. Often, department chairs experience stressful situations because they have not tapped into the power of automation. To run a department smoothly and with as few headaches as possible, it's important to create a digital workflow with automated processes. Creating a digital workflow will simplify processes and ensure a time stamp. Here are a couple of example situations in which automation can come in handy:

- A department chair in a small department who was also in charge of making sure that all graduate students filled out a program of study appropriately found herself pressed for time. She worked with her staff assistant to come up with a checklist for students with a process document and a template that allowed the students to fill out their program of study (POS), check their work, and submit it online. The chair also trained her staff assistant to check for inconsistencies in the POS that could prevent safe passage of this type of paperwork to the next level.
- Deans constantly ask for information about faculty and departmental achievements. While there is always a set time during the year when

reports are due with this type of information, a department chair needs to always be prepared to provide this information. A reactive chair waits for a request from the dean and then sends an email to the faculty asking them if they have any information to report. Faculty members typically ignore such requests or make it a low priority to respond, so the chair will have little information to report back to the dean. However, a proactive department chair knows the pulse of the department and collects information on a regular basis. This means that the chair needs to be in the habit of regularly collecting information about what's happening with the faculty and students. A good way to do this is by having a brief "kudos" session at faculty meetings where faculty can share a brief statement about their recent accomplishments or accolades. Your AA can follow up with each person who shares to gather more information as needed.

One faculty member shared the following thoughts regarding how his department chair automates processes. *"My department chair is a pretty forward-thinking individual. He makes sure that he knows what is going on with the faculty members and the students. He talks to us formally and informally, and even his hallway conversations are interesting. I can tell that he is constantly collecting information to report upward. He really removes the administrative burden, and he does not simply forward emails from the dean and others to us and tell us to respond. He only sends us emails if he really needs information. I like this approach because I really do not have time to respond to every forwarded email! I feel comfortable that he is taking care of departmental affairs and looking out for us."*

Leading faculty meetings

Faculty meetings can allow you to set the tone for your leadership style. In these gatherings, all faculty can see how you communicate and how you interact to build consensus (in some cases) and make decisions about important departmental affairs. It is essential to establish a regular schedule for faculty meetings—especially in the beginning stage of your tenure as chair. Usually once a month provides a good cadence to let faculty know about important affairs and discuss issues and upcoming activities. Often, I field questions from early-career chairs about how to conduct faculty meetings. Here are some guidelines I suggest:

> Tread carefully when selecting a set day, time, and frequency for faculty meetings. The first Tuesday of every month may work well for your schedule, but how about your faculty and staff? Of course it's impossible to satisfy everyone, but try polling several folks before settling on a routine. Also, it's a good idea to map out major conference dates, university events and deadlines, and holidays so that you can avoid as many major conflicts as possible and boost attendance.

- **Have an agenda for the meeting and send it out a week in advance.** This gives faculty an opportunity to let you know if there are items that they would like to discuss, and you can add things to the agenda as needed.

- **Make sure that meeting days and times are consistent.** Ask your AA to find a time at the beginning of each semester so there are no conflicts related to faculty teaching schedules and standing meetings on your calendar. Consistency allows both you and your faculty to plan around these time blocks.

- **Start your meetings on time whether all faculty are there.** I realize that voting decisions need a quorum, but faculty need to be in the habit of showing up on time. After all, they expect their students to show up on time for class.

- **Review highlights from the previous faculty meeting.** It is always useful, much like teaching a class, to review the major items from the most recent faculty meeting, including action items and meeting minutes. Try to keep this part brief, and only mention the most important items. The majority of the meeting time should be devoted to new topics.

- **Items that are important and require discussion and voting should take priority.** (Arranging the meeting this way also provides extra motivation for faculty to be on time!) More informational items can be at the back end of the meeting. and even if you must end the meeting before discussing those items, faculty can read more about them later if you make your meeting slides available.

- **Create a common, accessible e-folder for all meeting materials.** Place all slides, documents, handouts, and external links in this folder, and label everything appropriately. This will be a boon for new faculty members to learn about previous and ongoing department activities.

- **Ask your AA to prepare notes in the notes section of the meeting slides.** Your AA should always be present in faculty meetings, so he or she can take notes and add them to the slides either in real-time or after the meeting. Be sure to review these notes and approve them so the AA can post the slides with notes and action items. Either you or your AA should send the faculty an email notifying them when the meeting information is available. If any faculty members were unable to attend, they will be able to review the slides and notes to catch up on what they missed.

- **Every faculty meeting should include information about what is happening at the college and university levels.** As chair, you will participate in meetings that the dean has with other chairs (probably monthly). The dean will likely share information that she acquired from other deans and university administrators, and some of these items should be shared with your faculty. (Always clarify with your dean what is appropriate to share broadly with faculty and what is not.) You will play a critical role in facilitating information flow throughout the administrative chain. Your job is to ensure that faculty are informed about programs, initiatives, and policies that affect their jobs.

- **Keep meetings on track.** Faculty meetings should stay on task but also allow for healthy interactions among faculty on important issues. It can be a delicate balance to attain each time. If discussions steer off-topic or a presentation goes on too long, then you need to take charge and steer the conversation to its intended place. Like teachers often do in the classroom, you may even have to ask your faculty to save their "sidebar conversations" for later to reduce ambient chatter. This is an important skill to learn and master. Otherwise, your faculty meetings will be too long and tiresome, and faculty will find excuses to leave early.

- **Start with the "good stuff."** It's always nice to kick off meetings on a positive note, so I suggest starting faculty meetings by announcing any recent awards and accolades earned by department members. There will almost always be something to share. Keep this congratulatory segment brief but sincere, then move along to other agenda items. If you talk with your faculty on a regular basis and keep them informed about important developments, then faculty meetings are often short because most of them are already familiar with the items you share. It is also important to give periodic updates on the budget (which can be at the end of each semester) including what the recent expenditures look like and what the expectations are for upcoming financial matters.

Recognizing the accomplishments of your faculty helps everyone feel more like a team.

- **Follow a standard set of voting rules.** When it comes to voting matters, be crystal clear on how voting will proceed. Robert's Rules of Order is a widely used standard that works well for managing voting processes in faculty meetings. Here is an example of how Robert's Rules of Order could be used in a typical scenario:

Faculty Member A: *I move that we remove this course from the catalog.*
Faculty Member B: *I second the motion for discussion.*
  (Another member of the group must second the motion or the motion dies. It is good practice to discuss all matters that are necessary.)

Department Chair: *The discussion on this matter is concluded, so now we will vote. You may vote Yes, No, or abstain from voting.*

This was an example of a simple voting situation, but there are several other details to consider. First, there are different types of motions that can be made. A "main motion" must be made and seconded to initiate discussion on an issue (a limited amount of discussion may be allowed at the discretion of the chairman prior to a motion being made). Motions should be projected onto a screen for all to see before being voted on. A "substitute motion" is used to propose an alternative action to the main motion. Up to one main and two substitute motions may be on the floor at one time. If a substitute motion passes, it does away with the prior motions. If it fails, the previous motion comes back up for consideration.

Something called "friendly amendments" can also be introduced, which are editorial changes that may be allowed if nobody objects. However, any member may object and deny such requests. "Call the question" is a motion that ends debate and urges a vote on the motion at hand. If seconded and passed, the main motion is then voted on. If there is no second or the motion fails, discussion continues. (At any time, the chair can choose to end the debate.) If someone makes a "motion to table," then like "call the question," this is a motion to conduct other business and revisit the topic later in the meeting. A subsequent motion to "take from the table" is required to reopen discussion. A "motion to reconsider" can only be made by a member on the prevailing side of a previous vote. If seconded and passed, it rescinds the previous vote and brings the motion back into discussion.

- **Be clear about voting methods.** Sometimes different voting methods may be used during faculty meetings, but I recommend choosing one method and sticking with it in most cases. Here are the main options:

  - **Adopt by consensus.** This method works well if there is no opposition or only one or two opposed.

- **Voice vote.** This is a straight "yes" versus "no" vote, and voters state their vote out loud. If you predict that a vote will be close, this method can be difficult to use.
  - **Show of hands.** Keep hands raised until the chair and staff have completed counting for a "yes" versus "no" vote.
  - **Roll call vote.** Only use this method if it is requested by a voting member. Every person present will be named and asked to state their vote out loud.
  - **Secret ballot.** This method is only used to elect Chair and Vice-Chair in a voting group.

- **Take steps to encourage attendance.** Depending on the agenda items, faculty meetings can easily run long (more than an hour). However, if you have regular monthly meetings, you will avoid having to schedule inordinately long meetings once a semester. The goal of the faculty meeting is to get all faculty in one place at one time so that relevant issues can be discussed, and department members can build rapport with each other. Otherwise, getting faculty to socialize to build team

An appetizing buffet of snacks is usually a successful way to encourage meeting attendance.

morale is often difficult. I know a clever chair who provided refreshments—really good refreshments—at least 30 minutes before the start of the meeting. Once word got out that these refreshments were indeed excellent, faculty members were much more inclined to venture out of their offices to have a snack and converse with their colleagues. Faculty meeting attendance also improved, and the meetings began at the correct time. Well played!

- **Establish committees when the need arises.** Sometimes one comment leads to another and another and another, and soon you have a major debate on your hands concerning a particular issue. Discussions that clearly require more time should either be shifted to another faculty meeting, or a committee can be formed to research and address the issue. Typically, the department chair discusses the need for a committee at a faculty meeting where she outlines very clearly the mandate, responsibilities, and expected outcomes of the committee's work. A committee usually has a committee chair and three to five members, depending upon the size of the department and the nature of the committee. The chair should ask for volunteers or nominations for the committee chair and for members. Typically, faculty will volunteer to serve on committees but may be a bit reluctant to serve as committee chairs. This is where the persuasive powers and leadership of the department chair become necessary to encourage faculty members to take on a temporary leadership role. It is also a good practice to have a "policy document" which clearly outlines how committee members are selected and the length of the term.

Productive faculty meetings always include an agenda with clear goals, especially if faculty voting is required on certain matters. Discussion should be inclusive, and meetings should not drag on forever just because someone wants to hear themselves talk. Just like a skilled teacher, think of ways to encourage comments and participation from all your faculty members. Be sure that meeting notes are thorough and made available for faculty no more than a day after the meeting, and archive all information in easy-to-find electronic folders.

Establishing a seminar series

A vibrant seminar series in your department can meet various needs, but first and foremost it allows your students and faculty to see the breadth of research happening around the country. Whether you come from a department that has a seminar series for students and faculty or not, it is imperative that you establish one in your new role if it does not already exist—especially if you have graduate level programs. In a mature, well-established department, a seminar series usually exists already, and faculty are periodically asked to invite their colleagues to give seminars and interact with the students. Even if the department you are inheriting has a seminar series up and running, you can review the program and suggest some changes. Below I've outlined some best practices for establishing and maintaining a successful seminar series.

- Depending on your seminar budget, you can not only invite speakers from around the country but also from around the world who will provide an international perspective for your department.
- Seminar speakers should be as diverse as possible. Even if your department is a bit narrow in its degree offerings, inviting speakers to come discuss a wide variety of research topics will be informative and maybe inspirational.
- As department chair, allow students to share input about who to invite for seminars, and provide appropriate advice on what will benefit the department.
- Most departments have a budget to help cover the costs of inviting speakers to campus. It is always beneficial if the speakers spend an extra day or two on campus rather than just flying in to give a seminar and immediately going home. This extra time can increase collaborative efforts.
- You should commit to giving a talk every academic year or even every semester and provide an update on departmental and university affairs

Gather student input about who could be invited to give a seminar.

—from enrollment, awards, and student and faculty activities to the scope of research being done in the department. This provides the entire student body and faculty with an excellent summary of current affairs. Make sure that you invite key stakeholders to your seminar so they can appreciate the work that is being done in the department. Side note—your seminar talk can be easily adjusted for when you travel to other venues and universities for recruiting and branding purposes.

- Seminars are an excellent opportunity to invite faculty from outside your department to share their work to see if there could be interdisciplinary, collaborative opportunities between your department and theirs.
- Establish good practices for seminars. Speakers should be introduced properly, and either you or the seminar coordinator should moderate the discussion afterward. Needless to say, as department chair, you must attend all of these seminars unless there are extenuating circumstances.

Department celebrations

While the work of a department chair never stops, celebratory events and holidays should be downright fun. Scheduling social time for your faculty and staff that is not driven by an agenda is an important way to foster collegiality and morale. Planning these events is also a way to empower your AA. You can share your general thoughts but allow her to take the lead and "own" the events. Let's use a year-end celebration as an example.

- The biggest priority is to make sure that as many of your faculty, staff, and students as possible will be there. It is also important that you invite the appropriate personnel to campus. Even if they cannot attend, you should also extend invitations to other personnel on campus that you and your staff regularly interact with like admissions staff, graduate student office staff, and the dean.
- Don't be afraid to show some enthusiasm! If you are not excited about your event, then no one else will be. As chair, it is your responsibility to set the tone for the event, so bring it up in conversations with those who you have invited and let them know that you are looking forward to the celebration.
- Adopt a "service" role at the gathering. Show up early to help set up, and don't leave before the event ends. Having the chair stay until the end and even assisting with cleaning up speaks volume to your AA and everyone around you.
- Even when you are in a more social mode, remember that you are still viewed as a leader. Be prepared to welcome people to the event and perhaps plan a few remarks to share after most people have arrived. One department chair that I know had a PowerPoint scrolling on a projector screen with student and faculty accomplishments and photos from the year.
- Don't skimp on food at events like this! Make sure that you provide appropriate options (e.g., vegetarian, vegan) for everyone in attendance. If

you are an omnivore, be sure to familiarize yourself with good options for those with more restrictive diets. An administrator I know always served non-vegetarian options at his events until he received feedback that some would prefer other choices. He was happy to oblige, but in his eagerness to announce his vegetarian "dish" his email said, "This year we will have humus for vegetarians!" Several faculty members promptly sent him the definition of humus and told him he probably meant hummus!
- Year-end events are also a great place to invite donors for your program. The vibrancy and the excellence of your department should impress your potential and current donors.

The beginning of the year is also a great time to organize a social event. For example, you could plan a luncheon for incoming graduate students. This would be a great time to explain how processes work in the department, who the points of contact are, what the differences are between GTAs and GRAs, roles and responsibilities, and how to manage and succeed in graduate school. After you share your presentation (try to keep it brief!), you can invite faculty, staff, and the graduate students to eat together and mingle.

Chapter 4 Summary and Questions

In this chapter we…

- **Considered how to get "in the groove" of being a department chair.** The goal for a new chair is to achieve a proactive, not reactive, status of addressing tasks and issues. For some people, getting to this point may only take a few months, especially if the department and university are smaller. For others, it may require much more time and effort to get a handle on all the events and deadlines that occur each academic year. Be sure to rely on your AA and other staff members to help you stay on track. The sooner you are informed about what you will need to tackle, the sooner you can manage your time effectively so that you can address your own research and personal projects.

- **Surveyed methods of managing your calendar, email, and digital workflow.** Organization, organization, and more organization is the key to staying on top of communication, requests, and tasks. This will require frequent communication with your AA, especially as you begin your role as chair. It will take some type for you and your AA to settle on a calendar and email management approach that works well for you both and doesn't allow responsibilities to fall through the cracks. Also, remember to automate processes as much as possible. Automation can ensure consistency and timeliness in accomplishing tasks.

- **Discussed how to effectively lead and manage faculty meetings.** Convincing a group of highly educated, opinionated, and busy faculty members to regularly attend faculty meetings and be actively engaged in the topics discussed is no small feat. You will need to juggle a lot of things at once when you lead these meetings—sharing relevant information accurately and concisely, moderating appropriately when discussions and votes occur, encouraging participation in department initiatives, and recognizing faculty accomplishments, just to name a few.

- **Contemplated ways to boost faculty engagement through a seminar series and department celebrations.** Often these "extra" events really become that glue that binds a department together. When opportunities are provided for faculty to learn something new from a guest speaker or celebrate their collective achievements in a fun, informal setting, you will find that people will develop a deeper camaraderie. If you go the extra mile to plan these events, then most faculty will certainly appreciate the effort.

Answer the following questions to learn more about how the chapter content applies to you personally.

1. Consider your average weekly workflow. Try to break down your work tasks into several categories (e.g., research, teaching, duties, etc.). On a scale of 1-10 with 1 being "never" and 10 being "always", how effectively do you feel that you manage your time/focus for each of these categories? What advice stood out to you when reading this chapter that could help you improve your time management?

2. Think back to faculty meetings that you have attended in the past. Were there any particular faculty meetings that you felt were managed well and were a valuable use of your time? If so, what aspects of those meetings made them uniquely successful and worthwhile? If you can't think of any "good" faculty meetings you have attended, what could have been done to improve those meetings?

3. Make a short list of seminar series speaker candidates whom you know personally. What specific insights could these individuals offer to your faculty? Is your list diverse and inclusive? What would it take to convince these potential speakers to travel to your university to speak?

Chapter 5.

Managing People and Relationships

T HE JOB OF A DEPARTMENT chair is truly multi-faceted. You will sometimes feel pulled in a hundred directions at once, required to use
all your skill sets on a daily basis. When the business of your schedule
becomes overwhelming, try to remember that connecting with and supporting the people you work with is fundamentally what your job is all
about. There are budgets to manage, curricula to monitor, and a host of
processes and policies to follow. All of these things will compete for your
time and attention, but take care to avoid allowing them to drain the
"joy" of leading people and developing relationships.

Some department chairs seem to have an innate knack for always
having time to chat with faculty and students, while other chairs struggle
to devote much time to building relationships. Regardless of where your
strengths lie in this area, you should know that this part of leadership is
often the most rewarding. You probably don't want to be remembered as
a chair who merely "administered" from a closed office through emails
and phone calls, only emerging to lead uncomfortably dull meetings. If
you aim to manage people well, almost all aspects of your job will truly be
easier. Therefore, forming authentic, genial, yet professional relationships
with your faculty is of paramount importance.

I heard a department chair in a rather small department say one time,
*"I find it inefficient to talk to faculty one-on-one in their offices. It seems like
a waste of time. I'd rather send an email or have a collective faculty meeting."*

To which I replied, "*Sure, it may be more efficient to draft an email, but you will never get to know your faculty or build any meaningful relationships that way.*" While you may or may not agree with the statements above, in my experience, successful and "happy" department chairs are ones who put forth the effort to interact with their faculty. Another department chair put this in a different way, "*I talk to my faculty regularly in informal settings. The perspectives that I learn from them help me to build consensus around larger issues. So, when I call for a faculty meeting, I know all their questions already regarding a certain topic and have tried to answer them in advance.*" I find this approach to be forward-thinking, but remember that this may not work in every instance and with every faculty member.

As you read this chapter, consider how you are naturally inclined to communicate with your colleagues, students, and administrators. Are you a "people person" who will have little trouble prioritizing relationships, or are you more content as an "office hermit"? Regardless of your personal characteristics, all leaders can benefit from some intentional reflection on how and why strong relationships among people are the bedrock of a successful organization.

Department cultures

The overall culture of a department is usually a good representation of the fundamental relationships among the people who make up the organization. Cultures can be inclusive and enthusiastic to downright toxic and everything in between. As department chair, you must not only know how to monitor the culture of your department but also how to foster a culture that enables everyone to work effectively. As you strive to manage people well on an individual basis, keep in mind that the relationships among your faculty and staff weave together to form an overarching impression of the department as a whole. What kinds of cultures are typically found in academic departments?

The A+ department. This department cultivates virtues of excellence, inclusivity, and effective communication. As leader, the department chair sets the tone for the quality of work expected and communication practices with students, staff, faculty, administrators, and other stakeholders. The faculty fully understand their roles and responsibilities and are effective instructors and researchers. They also know in what roles they should serve the department, the community, and the university. Problems are solved within the department in an amicable manner without resorting to unprofessional behavior. The students are active citizens of the department and work well with the chair and faculty to help accomplish departmental goals.

If this sounds like the somewhat unbelievable movie version of an academic department, believe me when I tell you that some departments actually do function at near-optimum levels. The department can even start to feel like a supportive family. If you think this type of culture manifests organically and is dependent upon the students and faculty to make it happen, then you are wrong. It is your responsibility as chair to lead your department in identifying and creating the type of culture that you collectively desire. If you inherit an A+ department culture, then consider yourself very fortunate, but don't just set the cruise control. You need to be watchful and mindful of the decisions you make. This is why having formal (and impromptu) meetings one-on-one and as a group is important—so they can hear your thoughts, and you can also listen to them.

The grade F department. Everything that you read about the aforementioned "A+" department would have taken years to develop with persistent leadership and consistent buy-in from faculty. Now let's focus on the opposite end of the spectrum. A department does not necessarily have to be completely dysfunctional to receive a grade of "F". But it is surely headed that way! Here are some ways you can spot a department with poor or toxic culture:

This happens more often than most people realize... a new department chair steps into her role and realizes that practically everything is "on fire." It's tempting to start writing up new policies and forming committees to address issues, but nothing is going to significantly improve without buy-in. It's worth the time to start by giving faculty, staff, and students the opportunity to voice their opinions and ideas. This can be done in town hall-style forums, small group meetings, or one-on-one, depending on the size of the department. People will understand that you can't fix everything all at once, and once they feel heard, they will be more open to the new ideas and approaches you put forth.

- There is very little communication from department chair to faculty or amongst faculty. The chair chooses to communicate only via email and almost never engages with faculty in meaningful conversations.

- Faculty meetings are confrontational and inefficient (when they actually occur), and nearly nothing ever gets resolved. You may have a faculty member who likes to ramble about a certain topic and how they did things "back in the day…" Another faculty member may always voice an opinion about every topic, no matter how inconsequential. While being respectful, the department chair must propel the meeting forward by gently interrupting and suggesting that some discussions be saved for one-on-one conversations. Faculty usually are civil, but when you have a rude FM interrupting others, you have to tell them to wait their turn until another FM finishes their train of thought. Rudeness, snide remarks, and inappropriate words and behavior should never be tolerated. As chair, you need to develop the skills and tactfulness to address and defuse these situations.

- Staff assistants are not empowered to do their work successfully. If you tend to micromanage, your staff assistants will quickly pick up on this and let you do their job for them to avoid conflict. An exasperated dean told me once, *"It does not matter what type of document it is or what level of detail is needed—every time I submit a document to the provost, she would make numerous corrections using track changes. I was so fed up that I told my administrative assistant to start accepting all changes in the document and not fight that battle."* A classic case of micromanagement! You need to allow staff assistants to make the appropriate level of decisions so that they are empowered to assist you in departmental matters.

- Processes are poorly handled at virtually every level. A chair who has never spent time learning and administering processes is bound to frustrate everyone—from the staff assistant, students, and faculty all the way to the level of the dean's office. It is the responsibility of the department chair to know every departmental and college process and to make sure that it is followed correctly and consistently. Deadlines are there for a purpose, and providing exceptions will only complicate matters. Never let your staff assistant bear the brunt of the blame for lack of processes in your department. You are the department chair, and it is ultimately your responsibility!

- Student morale is low, and students do not work with the department to address issues and create goals. This is a clear sign that something, maybe many things, within the department are not functioning well. Involved and empowered students are generally content, so disengaged students are indicative of larger problems. Meeting collectively with students in your department (or a representative group) at least once a semester may be useful in reducing miscommunication and giving a formal opportunity to raise issues. Students who are empowered can be great allies for recruiting and helping with departmental events and initiatives, so take the time to listen to them, address their concerns, and get them involved.

- There is no strategic vision for excellence in teaching and research. While some department chairs think *"Well, my faculty have PhDs, so they should know how to do research and teach"*, that is a precarious assumption. While faculty have certainly taken their fair share of classes and performed considerable research, most will still benefit from mentorship and role models in these areas. As department chair, you have an excellent opportunity to set the tone about what constitutes excellence. This can be accomplished formally through faculty evaluations, but it should also be part of an ongoing conversation about improving pedagogical approaches and research practices.

- Finally, the department chair plays the "blame game." She often complains to the dean about the faculty then turns around and complains to the faculty about the dean! She doesn't take ownership of issues or actively seek solutions, instead opting to point the finger at everyone else when things don't go well. You can guess that this approach negatively impacts the whole university and doesn't bode well for a department chair's longevity. (You can read more about the "blame game" later in this chapter.)

The list of things that can go wrong in a department is endless, but I hope you get the point. It is the chair's responsibility to always monitor the culture and the morale of the department. Any time that a significant problem comes to light, the chair should take it seriously and be proactive about finding a way to achieve resolution.

Now, most departments will fall somewhere between the "A+" and "F" ends of the spectrum. Some aspects of how a department functions and how people interact will be healthy and productive, while other aspects could use some adjustment and guidance. As chair, you can have a strong influence on shaping the culture of your department. The next sections will delve more deeply into the opportunities you can take to achieve positive change within your department.

Leading by example

There are myriad ways of applying the advice to "lead by example." You can lead by demonstrating consistent professionalism, timeliness, attention to detail, and reliability. Also, two particularly important ways of showing your faculty that you are "in it" with them are continuing to teach and continuing to conduct research activities while you are chair.

Research. If you plan on being a research-active department chair, then it is imperative to carve out some "sacred" time during each week to purely devote to your research endeavors. As a professor, you may have had several students, post-doctoral researchers, and other research staff that allowed you to write many proposals and research papers, travel to conferences, and build a strong portfolio. Or perhaps you had a smaller team or no team at all and you pursued funded or non-funded research. While some of your research activities may have to be scaled back when you are chair, if you still retain a passion for research, you should absolutely make time for it in your schedule. I believe this is a good thing to do—to stay research active at some level. There are a couple of advantages to maintaining your research:

- It signals to the faculty that you are leading by example and to others, including the dean, that you are interested in staying relevant in your field. This means you will also be able to relate to the joys and disappointments of winning and losing grants. One chair put it this way, "*Yes, I teach, do research, write proposals and papers, and serve as chair. I give my faculty no excuses to slack off in any aspect of their lives.*" This is an extreme "leading by example" style, but for this chair, it works.
- Another advantage is that if ever you decide to leave the job as department chair, then the transition back to research is reasonably seamless. You may still need to rebuild the productivity that you lost while you served as chair, but at least you stayed connected and up to

date with your field. Here is what one chair had to say, "*Since I was a research-active department chair who was writing papers and managing my own research time, most faculty quickly figured out that there was no sense in complaining about the difficulty of research processes. They could not look me in the eye in earnest and complain about their research because I was pulling double duty as a professor and chair while still conducting my own research.*"

Everyone's calendar fills up a little differently, but here are some tips for managing your time so you can still make research a priority:

- **Coordinate and communicate with your AA.** Let your administrative assistant know that you intend to regularly schedule some time on your calendar for research. It is best to avoid being in your office

Sometimes it takes considerable commitment and effort to spend time on your research endeavors.

during these hours. Some department chairs have the luxury of having another office where they can "hide" to focus on their research. Others do this at home, at a coffee shop, or tucked away in a quiet corner on campus. Wherever you choose should be a space with few distractions, and try to put away your phone and avoid looking at any emails or documents related to your role as chair. It's a good idea to let your AA know where you plan to be during this time in case you are truly needed. You can work out the details as you go along, but the most important thing is to set a time for research on your calendar that your AA guards fiercely. Taking time for research and being productive during that time to accomplish your goals may not go according to plan at first. It may take a while before you find what works best for you.

Here's how one chair aimed to continue his research. *"Carving out time for my research every week in a location other than my department chair office was crucial for me. Having this time devoted to research allowed me to breathe easier, and I felt that I could think more clearly. I had to work hard to not open chair-related emails or answer phone calls in this time frame. If there was an urgent matter my AA knew where to find me. Other than that, I was completely firewalled for that time."*

- **Your time will not always be "yours."** Even though you may set aside time for research, it's quite possible that this time will be encroached on by other pressing responsibilities. Your responses, signatures, and attention will simply be required at times that conflict with your best laid plans to "deep dive" into your research. However, there is no sense in getting frustrated because this is just part of being a department chair. No matter how well you coordinate with your AA and other department members, you will not always control all aspects of your job.

- **Mentor someone on your research team to adopt a leadership role.** Sometimes an extremely active researcher becomes a department chair. They likely have a strong research team with multiple researchers and graduate students, a vibrant portfolio of grants and peer-reviewed papers, and frequent invitations to present at meetings and conferences.

University administrators often pursue these types of professors to head a department because they notice their leadership skills and they think their work will bring recognition and funds to the university. However, these universities simply assume that this person can easily do the job of a department chair and continue to conduct research at the same level as before.

I often recommend that if you have a sizable research team and are successful at managing this team, you should seriously weigh the advantages and disadvantages of becoming a department chair. Your vision may be exactly what the department needs, but you have to recognize that you cannot do both jobs as effectively as you would like and as well as others will expect. Therefore, even before you contemplate becoming a chair, you should embark on a journey to mentor someone on your research team who you plan to mostly (but not entirely) take over day-to-day operations if you become chair. It is now important to find the right person to be the first point of contact for research-related matters. This does not mean that you are relinquishing your role as Principal Investigator—after all, the research community will not understand or appreciate your desire to be department chair. Instead, you are establishing a "second in command" role that will serve both you and this person well. Whomever you choose will get the chance to take on more of a leadership role and add that to his or her CV.

Everyone in your professional life will have expectations for your performance. The research community that funds your research anticipates the same prolific output as always; the department wants you to continue doing research at the highest level while also being a stellar department chair; and your research team will still need frequent input and guidance. Plus, do not forget your personal life that also demands attention and care! While balancing all these activities and expectations seems like an insurmountable task, with proper planning, you can accomplish the goals that you set. But you will need to be patient in this process of working with all these constituents because it may take a few iterations to figure out the best management approach.

- **Expect some changes to your productivity.** Do not get frustrated if your "usual" research productivity—however you measure it—takes a dip. It is only natural for this to happen because you are now, in essence, taking on another job. In time you will learn how to adjust your metrics and perspectives to make all aspects of your professional and personal life work well. Set realistic goals for you and your research team when it comes to research productivity. Your team needs to know that you may not be able to attend every research team meeting and travel to all conferences at which team members may present. Assure them that maintaining a commitment to active research is a high priority for you, though.

Teaching. Much like leading by example through maintaining your research activities, continuing to teach classes is another important way to stay connected to students and faculty. You may not be able to teach every semester or teach many different classes, but even if you can teach one class per semester or in an academic year it will keep you relevant in the classroom. You will know students better and understand how to help them succeed. Usually, administrators who have distanced themselves from the classroom can only talk about increasing retention and student success, but they really do not understand the fundamental problems that students face and the difficulties involved in helping students achieve their goals.

A provost once lamented, *"We have so many places on campus to help students with math—student success centers, tutors, office hours—but they almost never come to these help sessions and continue to make poor grades and fail these courses."* This is a classic mismatch of designing programs to help students but never putting effort into figuring out how to best serve their needs. Teaching while serving as a department chair can be a crucial way to build an information pipeline between students and administrators which can lead to more confident and successful students.

Also, you need to be ready to fill in to teach a course when it is not possible to find adjunct faculty or if your faculty is already fully loaded. I know a department chair who was unable to find a faculty member to teach an entry level course because at the last minute someone pulled out of their teaching assignment. He taught the high enrollment introductory level course, setting an example for everyone in the department about prioritizing the collective good. Here's how one department chair kept one foot in the classroom: *"My college was looking for faculty members to teach a 'first-year experience' type of course for incoming freshmen to get them acclimated to the university. I quickly agreed to teach the course and helped with the curriculum as well. This was an easy way to get to know students at the very beginning and steer them towards my department."* Ulterior recruitment motive aside, this was an excellent way to interact with new students and answer their questions about the university and its programs.

Teaching also keeps you up to speed on the educational technologies that are available. Tools and platforms change rapidly, especially since online teaching has become more prevalent, so maintaining a basic awareness and understanding of these technologies is critical. Also, when one of your faculty complains about the available hardware or software, you can defend your position, not just with an assessment of the situation, but through first-hand experience. One of the biggest pushes on most campuses these days is to help students succeed by increasing retention and improving graduation rates. As an instructor, you will now have direct information that you can share about how to achieve these goals and the challenges that must be overcome to ensure success.

As part of your teaching and mentoring portfolio, it is also a good idea for you to mentor graduate students (masters and PhD) towards degree completion. One chair described how mentoring students was beneficial to her as well. *"Working with students kept me grounded and was a highly rewarding experience. Discussing research and motivating them to do their best research was always a highlight for me. I often encouraged them to write peer-reviewed papers, and I also provided travel funds for them to travel to conferences. At these conferences, I made sure that I introduced students to my spheres of influence. This felt right to me because, after all, I wanted to mentor the next generation of students in my area of expertise."*

Defending your faculty. Standing up for your faculty in certain types of situations is another way of supporting them and signaling to them that you understand their perspectives and goals. Thankfully, it is highly unlikely that you will have to "go to battle" for your faculty dressed as an ancient Greek warrior complete with shields and weaponry. Indeed, your faculty will make mistakes, say the wrong words at times to another administrator, be late on certain paperwork, etc.

A truly heroic department chair is ready to defend his faculty and staff when necessary.

Sometimes they will really need you to have their back, and it is your job as chair to support them and act if needed. Let's say that there is a hard deadline in your university for proposal submission so they can check, evaluate, and gather other pieces of information before sending them to funding agencies for review. If one of your faculty members is scrambling to complete a major proposal and submits it a few hours past the deadline and the proposal review office refuses to accept the proposal—you need to come to the rescue of the faculty member. Now, if this faculty member is perennially late and has taxed the system in the past, that's another story. However, if the faculty member is almost always punctual with other deadlines yet the research office is unwilling to relent, then you need to talk to your dean, the Vice President of Research, or whomever in the university to make sure that the proposal is sent to the funding agency. Defending your faculty in these types of scenarios is important for two reasons: 1) It is the correct thing to do, and 2) This is the type of chair you would want in your corner if you were faculty. If you remove some of the administrative burden of paperwork to keep things going in a positive direction, your faculty will respect and value your efforts even more.

Being accessible to faculty and students

Being accessible to faculty. Making yourself accessible to your faculty is important in the same way that faculty should be accessible to you for important conversations. Accessibility is built on mutual respect and is organic in nature. It can grow quickly or slowly depending on faculty social dynamics. Some faculty can be "high maintenance"—they like to wander into your office, and if you are not meeting with someone or not on the phone, they feel that you are free for a discussion. This faculty member may come in with one simple question but then expand the discussion to other issues. Sometimes these faculty members do not realize that, while they are at a point in their work stream where they can spare an hour or two for casual conversations, you may not be. Especially if you have an open-door policy, you should expect these situations to arise. In encounters like these when you really do not have the time to engage in extended conversations, you have a couple of options. After a few minutes of conversation, you can politely say that you are working on a deadline and would like to continue your conversation soon. Encourage the faculty member to schedule a time with your AA. This will signal to them that you really do value what they have to say. If your drop-by guest still does not take the hint that you are busy, tell them that you have until a certain time to talk with them (a few minutes in the future), but then you will need to return your attention to other duties.

Following an open-door policy can create an inviting, relaxed atmosphere, but it has its perils. You may have a faculty or staff member who always seems to be looking for someone to talk to. They wander the corridors with a coffee mug in hand, seeking anyone who will listen to their stories and ideas. Perhaps everyone tolerates or even enjoys these interactions, but over time, it may become an annoyance to some, which can make it a problem for you.

You have several different options for managing your own accessibility. You can choose to set up your office so that no one can even casually speak with you without going through your AA. The AA essentially "guards the fort." Depending on the size of your department, this could be the only solution that works, but I highly doubt it. If faculty feel that there are barriers to access, they may begin to view you as an unrelatable, disinterested administrator. There are, of course, formal meetings with faculty that should be scheduled and without interruptions. These could include performance review meetings or mentoring sessions for early career faculty members. These types of meetings are best held in a conference room (hopefully adjacent to your office) where you can have uninterrupted sessions.

Occasionally your attention will be required elsewhere, even when you are in the middle of a scheduled meeting. A college dean related a story to me about when he observed this sort of situation with upper-level administrators. "*I was in a meeting that the provost called for with deans of various colleges and two to three vice presidents. After a few minutes or so, the President of the university came into the room and gestured to a VP to come outside so he could have a quick conversation. He never knocked on the door or excused himself. The VP was absent for a few minutes and then came back into the room. Sure, there are sometimes urgent matters, but it is downright rude to interrupt a meeting with no apologies, even if you are the President!*"

Being accessible to students. In all the whirlwind of serving as department chair with meetings, faculty assessments, curriculum management, budgets, and raising funds, some chairs lose sight of the true end goal. The major reason that the department and the university exist is to train and mentor the next generation of students to take their places in society and achieve success in both work and life.

You can probably do the job of a department chair and not have personal interactions with students for long periods of time. Even when student issues arise, you may have an associate chair handle these issues. However, being accessible to students and listening to their concerns and ideas should always be something that you make time for in your schedule. Students have excellent ideas for recruiting, research, forming clubs, and other

> It's hard to overestimate the impact that you can have on a student's life. Giving a student a tour of your lab or guiding them towards helpful resources or programs can end up strongly influencing the trajectory of their professional career. As chair, it's easy to become bogged down in the daily minutia and neglect to focus on the main reason you accepted a job in academia. If you make it a priority to be accessible to students, you will never be sorry that you did. Their infectious energy will inspire you to do your best to support them, because the future truly depends on the choices they make and actions they take.

great ventures. Giving them your attention and support empowers these enthusiastic young men and women to be ambitious and creative. Here are a few practical suggestions for seeking ways to engage with students.

- If you have a graduate program in your department, then encourage your student body to select a graduate student representative to serve as the liaison between you (and faculty) and the student body. If they do not know how to start this venture, suggest some guidelines on the roles and responsibilities of this elected student representative and how long they should serve. Encourage this graduate student representative to bring items of importance to you regarding professional development, research, recruitment, and any ideas they have for student support and engagement.
- Students—especially graduate students—will truly appreciate being informed about departmental affairs. Here's what one chair told me:

"Once a month, I met with the graduate student representative to provide information about the items that the faculty discussed that are relevant to students. I also used this opportunity to gauge the pulse of the student body and to solicit ideas on how to continue to improve student morale."

- It is quite possible that there is a larger national organization relevant to your academic discipline that encourages local chapters. If one does not exist already at your university, assist your students in starting a local chapter. Examples of these could be local chapters of the American Meteorological Society, the American Psychological Society, or the Institute of Electrical and Electronic Engineers, among many others.

- As much as possible, invite students to attend conferences and cover their expenses with department funds. Smaller, more regional conferences might be a good place to start because they are less overwhelming and generally more affordable. Also ask students to attend recruiting events to represent your department. Potential recruits will especially want to hear from current students about their experiences, and this opportunity will give current students a sense of belonging and empowerment.

- Set aside funds for your graduate students to travel to conferences to present their research. Not all students may be funded by an adviser on grants and contracts, and some students will need the support of the department to showcase their research.

Here's an excellent plan that a department chair enacted to better inform graduate students about matters pertaining to them. Each semester the department chair set up a town hall meeting with the graduate students where the only agenda was to field questions from the students for as long as they would like and provide clear, transparent answers. The department chair noticed that a positive outcome of this meeting was that it considerably reduced misconceptions and "gossip". Once a student said in this meeting, *"We heard that student stipends are going to be cut because of university budget cuts. Is this true?"* In this case, the students heard some news and jumped to a scary, and thankfully incorrect, conclusion. The chair used this opportunity to explain in an easy-to-understand manner how universities function in relation to enrollment and student funding and was able to allay their fears. The chair also asked meaningful questions about how to improve student satisfaction and morale and how the department could help students succeed in research. Another student voiced that she wanted more information about traveling to conferences. In response, the chair put together a short workshop on conference opportunities and how to obtain funding. The ideas can be endless on how to engage students to foster a culture of inclusivity and excellence. However, as chair if you do not engage with students and merely choose to administrate via emails, then it is your loss! Information flow is vital to an excellent department culture. It also removes a lot of misconceptions about how the department and university works.

Being an effective listener

Listening to others around us is something we've all been taught since an early age, but department chairs should be masters at this skill. Some chairs are naturally good at listening, while others will need to cultivate and hone their ability to listen well. While academic administrators are often advised to be "effective communicators," very little is said or taught about effective, or what I like to call "active" listening. When you have discussions with faculty, staff, students, and administrators, an exchange of information will usually take place, but more importantly, the other person(s) will be seeking confirmation that they are being heard and understood. By being an active listener, you will glean as much information as possible from your conversations and assure your conversational partners that you respect and appreciate their ideas and views. Below are some practical tips for being an effective listener:

- When you meet with a faculty or staff member or a student, especially if this is a scheduled meeting to address action items, you need to make sure that you give your full attention to the other person(s). One effective strategy is to avoid sitting at your desk, so you are not distracted by your computer or stacks of papers. If you have a conference room near your office, then suggest meeting in this room instead. This tactic will encourage everyone involved to focus more clearly on the conversation.
- It should go without saying that answering your phone or texting during a meeting does not promote effective listening. Take a moment at the beginning of the meeting to put your phone into silent mode or simply leave it out of sight, if possible.
- Making eye contact and paying full attention to the conversation is critical. Your body language and actions should indicate that you are interested and invested in what they have to say. Here is what one faculty member had to say, *"My department chair is downright rude.*

*Putting your phone out of sight allows
you to be fully attentive in meetings.*

When I go to his office for a meeting, he sits at his desk with half of his body turned towards his computer and the other half to me. He glances at his computer while we are having a conversation and always seems distracted. Whatever I have to say never seems interesting enough to capture his attention. I absolutely hate going to his office." As extreme as that sounds, for some this is a reality. You will find little support as a department chair if you are not an effective listener.

• As department chair, you must find ways to navigate constant interruptions and juggle the variety of things that you are tasked with handling each day. Here are another faculty member's comments, *"A few minutes into every conversation with my department chair, her eyes seem to glaze over, as though he is not interested in the discussion we are having. Her mind seems to be anywhere other than the present."* As you meet with people, your mind will inevitably begin to wander to thinking about emails, upcoming meetings, your research, etc. You must be disciplined in not allowing your focus to wander or be broken by external factors. This is why you should take care to meet in a quiet, non-distracting environment. Try taking a pen and paper or digital writing tablet with you to jot down notes so you have a record of what was discussed, and you remain engaged in the conversation. Note any important action items so you can follow up on them later.

- Finally, it's good practice to reiterate portions of the discussion to reinforce important issues. Ask others in the meeting to verify certain facts or ideas to ensure that you have understood what they said. This tactic also demonstrates to others in the meeting that you are making every effort to listen carefully to their comments.

Overall, to be an effective listener, you should simply consider how you would like to be treated when you walk into someone's office for a meeting. Respectful, effective listening should become your natural approach.

Building spheres of influence

The first year of being a department chair will probably be a blur. There will be a lot to learn in terms of managing faculty, staff, and students; dealing with funding and budgets; conflict resolution; and a host of other issues. Probably the first time you get a taste of truly feeling like an administrator will come when you interact with other department chairs at the "chairs council" (when the dean meets with all department chairs). You should try to reach out beyond the council level, though, so you can learn more about how various parts of the university work and ultimately expand your sphere of influence.

There are numerous administrators at your university, and all of them may seem like they have disparate mandates. However, if you look closely, the university is (or should be) pulling in the same direction. The high-level goals at every university should look similar: educate the next generation of students in the best way possible, conduct leading-edge research to benefit the world, and serve local and larger communities. Yes, there is a business model that needs to be followed and executed, but the overall objectives are the same. Therefore, getting to know these administrators that support your department is worthwhile. This is what I call expanding your sphere of influence.

I know a department chair who absolutely hates to go to the chairs council, and he never interacts with any of the other chairs. He keeps his interactions with the dean to a minimum and scurries back to his office as soon as the meeting finishes. Granted, there is always work to be done as chair, but don't follow his example and waste a great opportunity to learn about the inner workings of the university. Also, expanding your spheres of influence will only produce more advocates for your department. Furthermore, if you have any intention of serving as an academic administrator at the next level (dean, provost, or vice president), these types of interactions will provide useful insight. Building these relationships does not mean that you are violating protocol by interacting with other administrators without the dean's permission. Here are some practical tips for building and increasing your spheres of influence.

- **Get to know your graduate dean.** Ask to meet her on campus for lunch sometime, and ask if she has ideas for increasing graduate enrollment for your department or better supporting current graduate students. Remember that the graduate dean has a travel budget for recruiting and has learned a lot on her recruiting trips. She is probably also well connected with other graduate deans around the country. While she may not be a subject matter expert in fields studied within your department, you can become an ally to the graduate dean in curriculum-related matters. Building rapport with your graduate dean also gives you some access to her spheres of influence. Sometimes these professional relationships can even turn into lifelong friendships.

- **Get to know your Vice President of Research.** If the faculty in your department conduct research with external grants and contracts from federal agencies, then it is important to build your sphere of influence with the Vice President of Research (VPR). He will obviously be very interested in meeting with you to learn about what new initiatives you might have to increase the research portfolio and revenue of the university. Therefore, the VPR will likely be motivated to provide seed funding for research projects that could generate a significant Return on Investment (ROI). Remember that the primary mandate of the VPR is to increase research revenues for the university, and your ideas to achieve that goal will ultimately benefit everyone from students to vice presidents.

- **Be innovative.** Quite often moving your department forward and securing more resources such as faculty lines could mean that you have to think creatively. Here is what one chair said about employing an alternative approach to meeting department needs.

"I got tired of writing justifications for faculty positions with data and more data, and I realized that my approach may be wrong. I joined forces

with a few other department chairs across the university that spanned liberal arts, business, science, and engineering. I put together a white paper outlining a new graduate program that cuts across multiple disciplines, but more importantly, I refined my ideas to attract the interest of national funding agencies such NSF, NASA, and DOE. Suddenly, the dean and several vice presidents wanted to know more about this proposal. The new initiative was seeded to obtain new faculty lines and write some omnibus proposals. It was a lot of work and sometimes exhausting but exhilarating as well. I was learning how to connect with faculty and department chairs across colleges and learning the language of funding agencies. Although the initiative was successful, it took a while to implement everything, so I had to be patient and continue to be the spokesperson for the project. Even if it was not funded, I would have learned a lot, but thankfully this was a success story."

Keep in mind that these are just a few examples of how you can interact with key administrators at a university. Fostering dialogue with administrators will help them understand your department better so they can help you achieve your objectives. Like so many times in life, success is partially determined by the people you know. So, make a good faith effort to get to know the people who can fuel that success.

Managing (up) your dean. Usually, the dean that you report to served a department chair at one time, and depending on the size of the college and your department, the job functions of a dean will vary. In larger universities, a dean's primary responsibility is to raise funds for the college. Most of the day-to-day work involved in running the college is left to the associate dean(s). This organizational structure is necessary because deans spend a considerable amount of time traveling and establishing relationships to raise funds. In other universities, fundraising efforts may be delegated to one central office on campus—usually called the Office of Endowment—and the dean will be more heavily involved in the daily affairs of the college. As I mentioned previously, getting to know your dean (and associate dean(s)) is critical for enabling good communication throughout the administrative ranks and seeking the best possible support for your department. So how do you manage (up) your dean?

- **Know the types of pressures that your dean is facing.** This means that you need to pay close attention in the chairs council meetings and also in your one-on-one meetings with the dean (which probably occur monthly). Listen for her to mention ways in which the college should improve. Some pressure for change may be coming from the provost (the dean's boss) or the president herself. Typical pressures that deans face are to increase enrollment to raise revenue, increase student retention (again, to raise revenue), increase student success and academic opportunities, increase graduation rates (which could even be a mandate from the state), increase the number of PhD graduates to raise the ranking of the university (usually to achieve R1 status), increase the number of research grants… I could go on and on. Your dean needs your help in facing these issues, and offering your assistance will ultimately help your department, the college, and the university at large.

- **Develop a professional relationship.** Hopefully your dean will make it a priority to regularly schedule one-on-one meetings with you. The conversations you have in these meetings should be meaningful and impactful, and they should also serve as an opportunity for you to develop a rapport with each other. You will spend most of the time in these meetings catching the dean up on department affairs. Sharing this information is important because no dean likes to be blindsided by problems. Aim to convey your news in a discussion-based fashion and not as a to-do list. You shouldn't feel the need to divulge everything that's happened in the last month; the dean primarily needs updates on the biggest issues in your department (like personnel problems) and will want to know about any recent successes. Keeping the dean informed is the best way to build a trusting, positive professional relationship with him.

- **Suggest a lunch meeting.** I know of department chairs who tried to meet with the dean at least once a semester in a more relaxed setting—

possibly for lunch. While the discussions are still centered mostly on the work of a dean and a department chair, a lunch meeting gives an opportunity for you and the dean to get to know one another in a more relaxed setting. Deans are a bit more inclined to talk about personal things like how they manage stress and the pressures they face in their position. It is never a good idea in these more casual meetings to lobby for a faculty position for your department or make a strong pitch for more funding. Deans almost always have a process they must follow with these requests and cannot agree to major requests with just a verbal affirmative and a handshake.

- **Advocate for your department.** As chair, it is your responsibility to ensure that your department's needs remain on the dean's radar. At the same time, you need to share the dean's thoughts and perspectives with your department members. In effect, you function as the

As department chair, you are the primary advocate for your department to upper administration.

information conduit between these two entities. Some messages will be easy and even enjoyable to relate, but others will be more complicated, and you will need to provide the context of decision-making processes.

Managing up, which means that you "manage" your dean by how you interact with him, does not mean that you just ask for resources (funds, faculty positions, etc.) without any cares about how the college operates. You should make a point to understand these systems so you can make realistic requests. At the same time, you cannot bash the dean at a faculty meeting to win the sympathy of your faculty. A good department chair can communicate effectively and honestly to both the faculty and dean while negotiating solutions that will benefit the department.

Sometimes being a department chair will feel like walking a tightrope between your dean and your department. One step too far in one direction can skew perceptions of you and the job you're trying to do. If you fail to communicate well with your faculty, they will start to think that you have become an aloof "administrator" and are no longer an effective advocate for the department. Alternatively, if you advocate for your department too strongly to your dean without considering potential big-picture impacts to the college and university, the dean will consider you immature in your role as an academic leader. This is why it is important to listen carefully to the dean about how and why she makes decisions. Even if your faculty don't agree with a particular decision, they will respect that you have taken the time to acquire a thorough understanding of how the decision was reached.

Knowing the pulse of your college and university

Have you ever heard the phrase "reading the tea leaves"? In case you haven't, it means "to use signs or signals to predict something that's going to happen in the near future." While not all chairs are adept at reading tea leaves, a lot can be accomplished by simply paying attention to what the dean is saying and keeping your finger on the pulse of the university. Here's an example of how one administrator was able to achieve success by being aware of university needs and resources.

A department chair made it a point to carefully follow news about various parts of the university. He noticed that the dean, president, and others were talking about how critical it was to increase student retention. Knowing that an accreditation team was about to descend on campus in a few months, he worked with the dean to develop a student success initiative designed to improve retention. The chair then identified the courses that had low student success rates and worked with the student success center on campus to develop a collaborative learning experience. He put together a committee led by a lecturer to work with the student success center to develop a curriculum that utilized creative pedagogical methods for diverse learners. As a result, student scores steadily increased in these courses, and at the end of the semester, the success rates increased significantly compared to prior years. The program was a huge success. It was quickly implemented by other departments across campus. Collaborative learning became a major theme across campus when the accreditation team arrived later. The department chair and his team garnered many accolades for this successful initiative.

The keys to this "win" for the department chair, students, and university was the chair's attention to the issue and initiative in addressing the problem. Opportunities like this exist throughout the university, so as department chair, it is important to stay tuned in to the affairs of the university.

> ## How can I successfully advocate for my department's needs?
>
> While a sparkling presentation and a flawless project proposal can go a long way in piquing the interest of university decision makers, there's only so much "pizzazz" that can work in your favor. Often the most important ingredients in your mission to fund new projects or acquire new resources for your department are two things -- timing and connections. Even if you pose what you perceive to be a reasonable request, remember that all administrators are constantly attempting to reconcile budget constraints with funding initiatives. If you know the pulse of the university, you will be able to time your requests most advantageously. Also tap into your sphere of influence to gather feedback about your advocacy approach and maybe some behind-the-scenes support for your department.

Knowing the pulse also means that you need to set aside some time to engage with your spheres of influence across campus. You can do this in more passive ways by reviewing the faculty senate proceedings, president's address, board of trustee reports, and the dean's initiatives. You will learn far more than you realize about the priorities and goings-on of the university. While this should not consume several days during a week, an hour or two of dedicated time is worthwhile. With everything that you learn, you will have a head start on knowing about any new programs and actions that are coming soon.

Usually when I ask department chairs what they want from their higher administration, I often hear statements like this: "*I want more faculty for my department, more resources (money and staff), more lab space, and more funds for graduate teaching and research assistants.*" But when I ask about how they plan to convince higher administration to give the green light to their requests, they aren't as clear. Below are two common opposing perspectives held by a chair and a dean about the needs of a department.

> **Chair:** *"Well, they owe us these faculty positions. We used to have more faculty at one time, and they didn't replace them when the faculty left or retired. Also, we need more funds for travel and teaching assistants to help with the courses."*

However, the dean over the same department may be considering other factors.

> **Dean:** *"Yes, they did have more faculty positions at one time, but they also had a lot of funded grants and contracts. They hardly have any research grants now, and they teach the same course load as they used to. Unless they increase their research portfolio, I am not going to provide more faculty lines. Yes, the number of GTAs is also less because we have limited funds these days for GTAs. Therefore, we expect faculty to step up and teach a little more."*

There is clearly a mismatch of expectations here, the dean will have more leverage in this situation. Maybe if the chair listens to the dean's feedback and implements some incentives for generating more research grant applications, the problem could solve itself.

As department chair, I have made the case based on data and strategic planning that we needed more resources. I also carefully prioritized department needs. I could have been greedy and asked for five faculty positions instead of two, but I knew that this approach would likely backfire. Therefore, I chose a phased approach of asking for faculty lines over multiple years. Sometimes universities with deep pockets, especially the ones that magically receive significant state or endowment funding, are in a good position to hire multiple faculty. In those envious situations, the dean may come to the department chair to start the hiring process for 5 or 10 faculty. Lucky you if you land a job at this type of university, but most universities will have tighter budgets with more constraints. While there may be a genuine need for several new faculty members immediately, there are usually not enough funds to accomplish this. Therefore, the phased approach that I used was successful because the dean saw that I was sensitive to the university's budgetary limitations but also had a strategic plan to grow the department as quickly as possible over time.

I followed the same approach to acquire more GTAs and GRAs for our department. I provided data to the dean that my faculty were indeed working hard to write proposals and secure grants, and I emphasized that it was important to support them in their endeavors. So, I proposed that we increase the number of GTAs and GRAs slowly to support faculty initiatives that would increase return on investment. I knew that I had to be reasonable and patient with my requests to stand the best chance of having them fulfilled. Being pushy and opportunistic in my approach would have only upset the dean and, in turn, made my job more difficult.

Don't play the "blame game"

At times, being a department chair may feel much like walking a tight-rope strung a thousand feet above the ground. It can seem like you have a great vantage point for everything, but the responsibilities can be over-whelming. Some aspects of being a department chair have to be learned the hard way, and others can be mastered with common sense and dis-cipline. One method of at least seeming to be in control is to exercise significant restraint in your words, actions, and emails.

One faculty member I spoke with described how she was disap-pointed by her department chair's attitude and comments. *"My chair is a downright negative guy. He starts every conversation by complaining about how busy he is and how hard his job is. To make matters worse, he always blames the dean or the system or the university for all his woes. Frankly, I am fed up with this type of attitude. I'm pretty sure he knew before he took the job that most things in academia are always moving targets, and these types of jobs can be stressful at times. Surely, he is being compensated well for being a chair, so why all the whining?"*

I'm sure you hope that no one ever describes you that way, right? Department chairs do not always have to be beacons of positivity, but remember that you reap what you sow: negativity breeds more negativ-ity! It is your responsibility to set the tone for your department. I am not suggesting that you "fake it" by acting as if everything is perfect, but you need to be careful about blaming everyone around you for the lack of progress in your department. As a leader, you need to understand that it is the job of a department chair to work through problems even during difficult times. Budgets may be tight and decision-making by upper-level administrators may be slow at your university, but it's your job to per-petually advocate for better processes and solutions. Complaining and whining about the job, lack of resources, or the dean will make you seem weak rather than someone to be pitied. Remember that you accepted this position knowing that it would entail challenges, and everyone knows that you are being paid to do the job.

If you are unsure about whether you have been complaining too much, it is rather easy to gather evidence. Take some time to sift through emails that you have sent to your faculty in the past few months. Now highlight sentences that seem like you are blaming someone else for bottlenecks, inefficiencies, and problems. If you find yourself highlighting statements from most emails, then you have been too busy pointing your finger at others. You can also talk to one or two senior faculty whom you know will tell you the truth. Ask them if you have been complaining too frequently, and hopefully they will give you the same answer that you reached by reviewing your emails.

Always aim for professionalism in your discussions with faculty and administrators. This doesn't mean that you cannot have casual conversations. You should just be aware that you are always representing your department. If discussions you have with others about your faculty might be considered gossiping or include even subtle attempts to cast aspersions on their integrity or their work, then you have to let go of this habit. You need to present your department and its staff in the best possible light, and always stick to truthful statements. Objective, data-driven assessments of your faculty are more important than mere anecdotal remarks about the skills and abilities of your team.

This may seem obvious, but avoid "playing favorites" with your faculty and staff. It is not a power move or a way to win votes in your favor. It's simply the beginning of a quick and deep slide to low morale in your department. Treat everyone with equal respect and professionalism so that no one feels ostracized. The last thing you want on your hands is a formal grievance filed against you for not treating a faculty or staff member with respect and that you did not follow equity and inclusivity guidelines.

Chapter 5 Summary and Questions

In this chapter we...

- **Discussed variation in department cultures.** A department's culture is heavily dependent on the ways in which people either do or do not communicate well. A well-functioning department can quickly degrade if communication among faculty, staff, students, and the department chair begins to falter. Chairs should aim to achieve an "A+" department culture, but depending on what kind of turmoil you inherit when you become chair, it may require considerable time and effort to make improvements.

- **Considered ways to positively shape the culture of a department.** The big three takeaways here are leadership, accessibility, and listening. Faculty members and staff will take their cues from *you* about the kinds of expectations that should exist in your department's collective professional environment. That's why you should make every effort to exemplify traits that you would like to permeate the department's culture. Making yourself accessible to faculty, staff, and students gives everyone the opportunity to be "heard", which is critical for building trust and cooperation. (And you'll inevitably gather some interesting perspectives and ideas through these interactions!) Even though you may find it difficult to carve out time in your schedule to be accessible to others, remember that truly listening to people effectively will go a long way towards creating department stability.

- **Emphasized the benefits of understanding your university's priorities and expanding your spheres of influence.** Many department chairs become so consumed with their daily responsibilities that they neglect to look much beyond the four walls of their office or building. The truth is that your department functions as a cog in the much bigger machine of a university, and it's important to recognize the implications of this hierarchy. If you want to be the best advocate possible for your department so you can secure funding and support when needed, build your spheres of influence by consistently attending college- or university-wide meetings and department chair events. You can network with other administrators and hopefully build relationships that will become both personally and professionally fulfilling. Attending these meetings (or at least reading the minutes) will also keep you "in the know" about your university's broader visions and priorities, which will help you tailor requests to your dean and other administrators to align with current ideas and concerns.

Answer the following questions to learn more about how the chapter content applies to you personally.

1. If you had to "grade" your current department culture, what kind of grade would you assign? What characteristics of your department influenced your decision? What do you think could improve your department's culture in the short term? In the long term?

2. Define your personal expectations for your research and teaching duties while you are department chair. Try to set concrete, realistic, and attainable goals. Ask a mentor or trusted colleague to review your goals and expectations and give feedback about their feasibility.

3. On a scale of 1-10 with 1 being "not at all" and 10 being "totally", how "in tune" do you feel with the students in your department? How often and in what ways do you interact with and hear from

graduate students? Undergraduate students? Do the students you meet with or hear from represent the majority of students? What steps could you take to increase student engagement with and participation in department-level initiatives?

Chapter 6.

Hiring and Supporting Your Faculty

Hiring new faculty should be an exciting phase during the tenure of a department chair. Forward-thinking department chairs align the strategic plans of the university and the college with the department and write strong justification about why new faculty lines are needed to support the department's stature and growth. This is an opportunity to unite faculty, students, and stakeholders to make a case to upper administration that will have long-lasting effects on the department. The faculty are the backbone of your department, so strengthening it is an essential part of preparing for a successful future.

A well-prepared department chair usually will get the administration's attention when it is time to decide which departments will receive funding for new faculty lines. If a department chair develops a detailed, thorough strategic plan and asks the faculty for their input, then the administration will take notice of the overall effort and enthusiasm within the department. This will likely influence the decision-making process in the department's favor. However, there may be various subdisciplines in a department, making it more difficult to gain consensus about which discipline has the greatest need for more faculty. Regardless of how they are acquired, new faculty inject youth, exuberance, and ambition in a department. While some faculty may be retiring or moving on to other ventures through this process, the legacy of a department chair is sometimes seen in the new hires. I even know of department chairs who reference their faculty hires as their greatest contribution to their departments and are very proud of the success and leadership roles that those faculty have earned.

In this section, I focus primarily on describing the various stages of hiring and what some best practices are for the steps involved. Several sections also address how to work with different types of faculty positions and how to establish successful mentorship for them. While the hiring process is exciting for all involved, it's paramount to build support systems and practices that bolster and empower all types of faculty members—even those who only set foot on campus to teach a single course.

Hiring faculty for your department

Most department chairs that I know want to leave a mark on the department, and one way they want to achieve that is by hiring new, dynamic faculty members. Depending on the department's structure, needs, and budget, faculty can be hired at multiple levels—assistant professor, associate professor (with or without tenure), or (full) professor. Usually, departments hire new faculty at the assistant professor level for various reasons. At this level, there is more of an opportunity to diversify the teaching/research portfolio of the department. Hiring assistant professors is also cheaper, and it often provides balance to a department that already has an abundance of associate and full professors.

Just like hiring a department chair, hiring new faculty members is typically a long, involved process. Many people and multiple units on campus will be included, so getting a head start is important. Remember, you will

Many department chairs leave their "mark" by developing new initiatives or acquiring new funding sources. These are certainly worthwhile ways to support a department. But consider that perhaps the most effective long-term success strategy is to attract and hire the best faculty you can possibly find. Incorporating new people into your organization provides a means of fine-tuning the course offerings, long-range goals, and research foci of the department as a whole. A single outstanding hire can positively influence a department for decades to come!

in essence be competing against other universities for the same talent pool. The more prepared and organized you are, the better your chances may be of hiring your first-choice candidates. Even if you end up with a fairly large pool of candidates and you have downselected the short list to five impressive applicants, you can still encounter issues. For one reason or another they could all—yes all—withdraw their application at the last minute even after you have already invited them to campus for interviews. If you did not start the hiring process early, then you won't have much time to go back to the applicant pool and identify a few more possible candidates. Additionally, while you may be given an opportunity to hire faculty for your department, if you fail to find a viable candidate, then funding intended for your hire may be diverted to another department.

There are several phases in a typical search and hire process. You should be aware of all components and about how long each phase will take so that you can adequately prepare.

The pre-advertising stage. Everyone is excited to interview a faculty candidate, but the pre-advertisement stage is critical and should be executed with great care. As department chair, you need to adopt a "hands-on" approach rather than simply allowing outcomes to play themselves out. With that in mind, here are some helpful guidelines:

- Make sure that you obtain explicit permission to hire from your dean in writing. Establish and agree upon an intended range for salary, startup, and moving costs and any other financial factors. Have the necessary conversations with the dean as early as possible to give yourself plenty of time.
- Assemble a hiring committee that is diverse, and do not be tempted to rush into setting up the committee by picking only faculty within your department or your senior faculty. A good committee should be comprised of members from various parts of the university, because they will each bring their unique perspectives. Ask a variety of individuals from your department, college, and the larger university if they would be interested in serving on the committee. Sometimes it

is even advisable to involve stakeholders as committee members because they can get the word out to their spheres of influence quickly.

- It is good practice to select a committee chair who can shepherd the process well from beginning to end. Keep an eye out for senior faculty who may be interested in this role, or you may be fortunate enough to have a reliable assistant department chair who can take charge. Sometimes the most obvious and best person for the role may be you, though. Even though the search and hiring processes may take significant time, you should know best what types of candidates would be the best fit for your department.

The chairperson of a hiring committee acts as the shepherd in complicated hiring processes.

- As department chair, it is ultimately your responsibility to ensure that all the paperwork is done properly. Do not delegate this responsibility to your staff assistant or the committee chair. There are many details and nuances in this paperwork that faculty and your AA may not be aware of.

- Avoid asking the committee to draft an advertisement for the job from scratch. Provide them with prior examples, templates, and your input about specific details to emphasize. You should be the one to edit and approve the final document and send it to the dean or whomever it should go to next.
- While only a subset of faculty can be selected to serve on the hiring committee, it does not mean that the rest of the faculty should be totally left out of the process. The best way to include the whole department is to simply create an electronic folder that all faculty can access. You can create subfolders for advertisements, the CVs and application materials of candidates, and the short list of candidates with justifications. This ensures complete transparency in the process. However, most faculty do not have the time to be involved in the process and will trust the committee's evaluation efforts.

The advertisement stage. A strong job advertisement is critical. It needs to not only capture the needs of the department but also the excitement for the position. You should also highlight the college, university, and local community, if possible. Job advertisements come in many forms depending on where they will be advertised. There will often be word limits in certain publications, so several versions are important. Featuring the advertisement prominently on your department web page is a smart move because you can add as much relevant information as you like. Again, it's very important that you advertise in multiple places with the mindset that you will reach a diverse set of candidates. That means getting out of your comfort zone of only advertising in a few journals that you know well!

Only placing advertisements on websites, in journals, and in other written forms is usually not enough to attract a significant pool of applicants. You need to aggressively recruit by encouraging people to apply. This means that you should attend conferences to look for talented individuals who may be interested in becoming part of your department. It also means that you have to pick up the phone or use social media to "get the word out." To get the best results, commit to being an active recruiter!

The applications received stage. The deadline for applications has come and gone, and your hard work has paid off. You have an excellent pool of candidates to review to create the first short list of candidates. Your committee work has really begun at this stage. Carefully poring over CVs to decide on prime candidates for a short list is never an easy task because several factors must be balanced. Committee members must consider teaching needs in the department as well as candidates' research expertise and niches, overall work experience, and their involvement in the larger community. For example, let's assume that you are looking for early career assistant professors. The candidates who apply may vary significantly in their career progress; some may just be getting ready to graduate with their PhD, while others may have already worked several years as a post-doctoral researcher or are already assistant professors elsewhere. While it is important to let the committee do their work without micromanaging them, you should be clear with them about the department's needs and what characteristics an ideal candidate should possess. It is always a good idea to keep your dean updated throughout the process so he can report up to the provost if needed. Depending on the university, you may have to write justifications for each candidate selected for an initial interview and submit them to upper administration. So, be prepared!

The initial interview stage. Usually this stage includes "virtual" interviews in which the committee sets up video conferences with candidates to ask them some questions about their application. It always helps to have a standard set of questions to ask all candidates, but be sure to ask follow-up questions when relevant. As department chair, it's your job to make sure that this is a fair and equitable process for all candidates. After all the initial interviews are complete, the committee has the (presumably) difficult task of selecting several candidates to invite to campus for further interviews. Depending on university policy, only a certain number of candidates may be allowed to enter the next stage due to standard protocols or budgetary reasons. Therefore, selecting the strongest candidates for campus interviews is crucial. At this stage, it may be a good idea for the committee chair (or you as department chair) to call a "special" faculty meeting to discuss the search process thus far and the candidates who have been selected for on-campus interviews. You should be prepared to justify why these candidates are the best, given the available pool. This is also your chance to educate your faculty about the complex hiring process because they may not be aware of all the paperwork and effort that goes into hiring new faculty.

The campus interview. You will need to work closely with the committee chair (if this person is not you) to prepare to host candidates on campus. First, you should draft and provide an agenda format for the visits. This means that you need to decide who the candidate will meet and when/where these meetings will take place. It is easiest and most equitable for all candidates to follow the same agenda. Be sure to send the agenda to the candidates ahead of time so that they are aware of what their visit will entail.

You should schedule a one-on-one meeting for yourself and each candidate at the start of their first day of interviews. Even if the meeting only lasts 15-30 minutes, you will be able to set the stage for candidates about what to expect and answer any of their questions about the agenda. Also plan to meet with candidates at the end of their visit to debrief and inform them about what to expect next in terms of communication and decisions. Serving as a bookmark for the interview process is useful for you and the candidate. Of course, you can always build another meeting into the agenda to meet with candidates and discuss job-related matters.

A good interview schedule will include meetings with students, faculty (possibly over lunch), committee members, the dean, the provost, the vice president for research, the office of international engagement (if a work visa needs to be discussed), and others that you see fit. The candidate should also be asked to present a one-hour seminar that includes question and answer time. I also recommend scheduling dinner with the candidate at the end of day one to get to know the candidate in an informal setting. Other committee members may be included as well, as your budget allows. While it is next to impossible to control what faculty say in their meetings with candidates, as department chair you can be a role model of professionalism and positivity and encourage your faculty to follow your lead. Be sure to remind faculty that it is never a good idea to air "dirty laundry" during candidate visits.

Candidate ranking and selection. Assuming that you have only one faculty position open, then it is time to work on ranking candidates and deciding who will receive the initial (and hopefully final!) job offer. This is a very important stage in the hiring process, and your entire faculty will appreciate a meeting (not via email) on the selection process and justification. Once you and the committee have worked together to rank the candidates, it is time to work with the dean to draft the offer. Depending on the university, either the dean will take over the process at that time, or the dean may ask you personally to take the lead. Either way, making the offer and having a follow-up conversation with the candidate is the next stage. Usually, the offer parameters include a nine-month salary, startup costs, moving costs, and office and lab space. It is your responsibility to provide all the necessary information about the department and the university.

After the initial offer has been delivered, the candidate may want some time to think it over. Asking for time to consider the offer is reasonable, but I recommend that you lay out a response timeline. If for

After interviews are complete, either you or the dean will likely be in charge of ranking new faculty candidates.

whatever reason this candidate cannot accept the job, you will need to quickly communicate with the next candidate on the list. Assuming that job negotiations go well, and all details of the offer are settled, it is time to put the agreed upon numbers in writing. Draft a summary email to the candidate and carbon copy the dean and committee members so that everyone is in the loop.

The official offer letter usually includes a lot of "boiler plate" material that is required by human resources. Be sure to review the letter before it is sent to the candidate to be sure that everything is correct. Next, send the offer letter to the candidate and ask for their signature which represents their acceptance of the job. You should set a clear deadline for accepting the offer so that the process does not drag on any longer than necessary. If you started early and all stages of the process went swimmingly, then at this point you will be in the middle of the spring semester with plenty of time for you, your department, and the new faculty member to adjust before the fall! Be sure to inform the faculty about the hiring outcome, and you should think of a way to properly thank all members of the hiring committee.

Caveats. Not all faculty searches go smoothly, and there is no way to predict what might go wrong in the process. Below are a few common issues that may be encountered.

- The application pool was weak with very few candidates. This simply means that you have to regroup and ramp up your advertising tactics. Focus on active recruiting approaches instead of waiting on potential candidates to discover job postings.
- None of the top three candidates accepted the packages that were offered to them. It is quite possible that the offer package was not commensurate with other universities. You have to assume that the candidates who interviewed at your department are also interviewing elsewhere, and they could make decisions based primarily on the salary and benefits offered to them. You may have to convince the dean to allocate more money to your department's budget to attract quality candidates.

- The candidate does not want to start in the fall, instead wishing to defer the start date until spring of the following year. This is a difficult situation. Perhaps this request could be accommodated, but sometimes there is no other option but to tell the candidate that this is not a viable option.

Mentoring early career faculty

Your role as department chair could be even more rewarding if you serve as a mentor for faculty members just beginning their careers. Imagine that you worked hard to convince your dean to establish faculty positions for the department; you led efforts to recruit the best possible faculty for your department; and now they are here and ready to start their careers. Making it a priority to mentor early career faculty or the new hires in your department can teach both you and them quite a bit and foster important professional relationships. If you adopt the mindset that some of the early career faculty that you brought on board as assistant professors could become leaders and department chairs someday, you will bring your "A game" to mentoring. Here are some things to consider about establishing good mentorship:

- First, recognize that, as department chair, you are in a completely different career stage compared to the early career faculty, therefore it will take a while for your faculty to get to know and trust you.
- Mentoring must be genuine. This means that you must always have the best interests of the faculty in mind. You should never use mentoring opportunities to delegate tasks to other faculty or put them on committees that do not interest them. Do that once or twice, and you will completely break the trust factor in a mentoring relationship.
- Establishing trust between a mentor and mentee is critical. As a mentor, you need to be genuine yet purposeful, professional yet empathetic, and relaxed yet focused in these conversations. Sharing your professional stories always helps because you will become more relatable and accessible to your mentees.
- Resist the temptation to only provide a laundry list "to dos." Use these mentoring times to listen carefully, and ask open-ended questions that encourage mentees to reflect on their experiences and goals.

- You have to be patient in the mentoring process because of the chair-faculty difference dynamic. It does not matter how often you reiterate that you are on their side; they need to understand you and the department as a whole to find their bearings within the faculty ranks.
- Never pit other faculty against your new faculty. Never ever. This is not the place for you to discuss strengths and weaknesses of other faculty. This is unprofessional.
- While formal mentoring sessions are important for mentees to ask specific questions, do not discount impromptu hallway discussions and the occasional times of just wandering into their office with a cup of coffee for a quick "checkup" conversation.

Bringing your mentor a cup of coffee or a small gift is a great way to thank them for their assistance and advice.

- It is to be expected that early career faculty are focused on their teaching, service, and research performance. Make sure that you provide the appropriate advice, and follow up with them about any concerns.

Be sure to avoid offering personal opinions that are not backed up by university policy. An interim chair I knew once led an early career faculty astray by saying, *"Don't worry about writing a lot of grants and contracts, because funded research is not that important for tenure and promotion to associate professor."* The interim chair clearly did not have the best interest of the early career faculty in mind, because policies clearly indicated that one of the metrics used to assess faculty performance for tenure and promotion to associate professor was success with securing external funding.

- Know the faculty and/or departmental handbooks well enough that you can steer your mentees to specific sections when needed. This will save them a lot of hassle searching for information and will also show them the importance of abiding by university policies.

- Finally, recognize that sometimes it can be difficult to establish a strong mentor-mentee relationship with some individuals. Whether it is the chair-faculty dynamic or other reasons, some faculty may not wish to "open up," causing discussions to be strained or non-existent. With the best interest of the early career faculty member in mind, you might recommend that an established faculty member serve as mentor instead.

Coaching associate professors

Sometimes there may be an associate professor or two in your department who are unsure how to progress to the next phase of their academic careers. As academics, we often expect everyone to "go it alone" and "figure it out." After all, we were capable of earning PhDs, which connotes that we should know how to teach, do research, and serve the university and the wider community successfully.

There is usually much excitement when a new faculty member is brought into the academic enterprise of the department. Maybe these early career professors are mentored well, and after a few years, they are promoted to associate professor with tenure. Most mentoring stops at

It's not unusual for academic careers to sometimes languish a bit. As a leader and a mentor, it's important for you to be tuned in to your faculty's successes and especially their struggles. If you have already established a solid baseline relationships, then faculty who are encountering difficulties will be more likely to both seek and accept your advice. Remember that we all need career mentorship along the way -- no one should be expected to figure it all out on their own. And as a mentor, you don't need to solve everyone's problems for them. However, you can be a beacon of encouragement to a faculty member who is floundering and help them create a plan to get back on track.

this stage, and the general sense is that these associate professors know what to do next. Many new associate professors will have a strong sense of what they want their next major career pursuits to be, but others may feel a little lost or stuck. Maybe their research grants have started to dry up, and students have begun to leave the research team. Perhaps a life situation has been negatively affecting the associate professor's work. Whatever the situation may be, one year becomes two, then a few more years go by, and the associate professor who excitedly began the next phase of their career is now disillusioned.

As department chair, it is absolutely your charge to be aware of these situations and to encourage and motivate associate professors when they need some extra support. With that in mind, here are some ways to help associate professors develop to their full potential.

- First, find (or create) an opportunity to have a good overall discussion with the faculty member about teaching, research, and other duties and services. Listen carefully to their comments, and resist the urge to be immediately prescriptive about their situation. You should realize that it may take several conversations before starting to put together a plan of action.
- Let's assume that the distressed faculty member was once highly prolific in their research but lately has had difficulty winning grants and sustaining a full research team. Therefore, funds for travel are limited, and proposal writing has become a demoralizing chore. I have talked with many faculty who have experienced this type of situation. The win rate (number of proposals awarded to the number of proposals submitted) gets smaller and smaller for various reasons—increased competition, reduction in available funds, and much more. Some associate professors will allow their win rate to dictate how they feel about the importance and success of their work. As department chair, it's your job to remind them that a single metric, while relevant, does not define their career.
- Department chairs have an excellent opportunity to provide encouragement and practical help with research. Depending on your area of expertise, you can write proposals with the associate professor where

she serves as a co-investigator. You can also connect the associate professor with other successful researchers to write peer-reviewed papers and proposals together. Encourage her to attend conferences where you can introduce her to your "spheres of influence" that include researchers and program managers. These new connections may inspire new research ideas and collaborations.

- As department chair, commit to setting aside some funds annually to invigorate research for faculty. Let all of the faculty know at a faculty meeting that this is one of your initiatives, so they understand how serious you are about providing this kind of support.

- Pay attention to the computing needs of these associate professors. Perhaps they need more powerful computers or servers or access to mainframes. Providing access to new technology will bolster their work and inspire ideas.

- Helping your associate professors to build success stories takes time, but with patience and proper mentoring, the journey for both you and them will be well worth it. It is quite possible that all an associate professor may need is for someone like you to offer encouragement and guidance.

Working with adjunct faculty and lecturers

Adjunct faculty. Often a department's teaching needs cannot be totally fulfilled by tenure-track and tenured faculty. Most departments hire adjunct faculty to teach "service courses" that fall within the department's purview. For example, just about any university student majoring in science, psychology, nursing, engineering, and business is required to take one or more mathematics courses. While engineering students may need a series of calculus courses, the college of engineering does not teach these courses. Instead, the university relies on the department of mathematics to teach these courses. Depending on the overall size of the university, these service courses could have hundreds of students, and the same can be said for introductory physics, sociology, chemistry, psychology, and other courses that are required to complete programs of study.

Using calculus as an example, we can see that sometimes it is difficult to have tenured and tenure-track faculty teach these courses. A few faculty may elect to teach some sections of introductory calculus, but most "research" universities prefer for more senior faculty to teach more advanced courses. Therefore, the department must hire adjunct professors or lecturers to teach many sections of calculus. In some cases, part time/adjunct faculty are hired from the local community to teach these service courses.

Another situation in which adjunct faculty are needed is if enrollment suddenly increases. The university may not have planned appropriately for the number of sections that must be offered, so additional adjunct faculty must be hired to meet demand.

In other departments, adjunct faculty may teach specialized courses. For example, if the department is just beginning to form courses in machine learning, an industry expert in the area may be willing to teach a course for one or two semesters to get the department started in the correct direction.

As chair, you will very likely encounter one or more of the situations described above that will lead you to hire adjunct faculty. When hiring and incorporating adjuncts into your department, there are several things you should consider:

1. Adjunct faculty credentials must match with the course that they are assigned to teach. Usually, adjuncts have a master's or PhD degree and work in a profession closely related to the course content they will present. They may or may not have prior teaching experience, though.
2. Do not delegate the process of hiring an adjunct faculty member to your staff assistant. You need to check their credentials and conduct an in-depth interview to ensure that they are a good fit for the course.
3. If the adjunct faculty member is going to teach large course sections, make sure that he has a graduate teaching assistant to help with the

Teaching assistants can support adjunct faculty by grading student work or leading tutoring sessions.

grading and tutoring students (if needed). Remember that he may have a full-time job already and is simply helping your department with a teaching need.

4. Make sure that you pay the adjunct faculty member appropriately. Sometimes the university may have strict guidelines about how much you can pay an adjunct based on the course level. However, there is still room to negotiate with the dean to offer higher compensation—especially if it is a critical course that needs to be taught.

5. While it is your job to ensure that a competent adjunct faculty member is hired, the faculty ought to be kept informed about the process and the person selected for the job. It's a good idea to occasionally ask your faculty to suggest potential adjunct faculty members based on connections they have in research and industrial communities.

6. Just like "regular" faculty members who teach courses, your adjunct faculty should be provided an office space, even if it's just a desk in a shared office. She will need to designate office hours for her students, so it's important that she has a space in which to meet with them.

7. The adjunct faculty member may be very new to teaching university-level courses or teaching at all. It is your responsibility to help them calibrate the course content to the department. Offer suggestions for a textbook or relevant reading material, provide templates for syllabi, and reduce the barriers to effectively using educational technology by ensuring they receive proper training for learning management systems (e.g., Canvas, Blackboard) and computers/projectors in classrooms.

8. Check in with the adjunct faculty member a few times throughout the semester to ensure that he is handling the course well. Offer suggestions regarding effective teaching and assessment methods, and be receptive to their ideas as well.

9. At the end of the semester, review the students' course and instructor assessments with the adjunct faculty member. This can be used as an evaluation to determine if you want to continue with the adjunct faculty the next semester, depending upon their interest.

10. Finally, it is important to treat adjunct faculty members with respect and make them feel welcome and included as part of your depart-

ment. Invite them to faculty events and meetings even if they only spend minimal time on campus.

Lecturers. Depending on the mandates and the teaching needs of your department, lecturers could play a significant role in the life of your department. If your department must teach large "service courses" (e.g., introductory math, psychology, chemistry) to fulfill the undergraduate general education requirements, then it may not be possible for only the tenured and tenure-track faculty to shoulder this responsibility. Tenured and tenure-track faculty typically must devote a significant portion of their attention to research-related activities. Lecturers, on the other hand, do not generally participate in research. Their only responsibility is to teach courses and perhaps serve at some minimal level on certain department committees. Here are some practical guidelines for successfully integrating lecturers into your departmental structure.

- It should go without saying that treating lecturers with proper respect is paramount. Never make lecturers feel that they are less valued than the tenured/tenure-track faculty members in the department. In fact, it is your responsibility to convey to the faculty that lecturers fulfill a critical need. These lecturers have large class sizes and spend many office hours teaching, training, and mentoring students to succeed.
- When hiring lecturers, make sure that you outline a clear process that involves a diverse group of faculty, staff, and other lecturers. As part of the interview process, you should ask lecturers to teach a sample class and interact with students. You should aim to hire confident, competent lecturers with excellent credentials who are invested in helping students succeed.
- Pay attention to the needs of the lecturers. Provide appropriate computers and tablets and any software they might need. Ensure that they are properly trained in using the equipment and programs by others in your department or the IT staff at your university.
- Stay engaged with lecturers throughout the year. One department chair I spoke with has a large contingent of lecturers in his department because they teach multiple sections of all the freshmen and sopho-

more level courses. Each year around the middle of the semester, the chair organized a celebration event to acknowledge the work of the lecturers (with a special lunch, of course) and listened carefully to the challenges they were facing. Often in these meetings lecturers voiced excellent ideas on how to improve course material and to better support students. The department chair also provided training opportunities for these lecturers and funds for them to travel to workshops and conferences.

- Always keep in mind that lecturers have an extremely high course load. Therefore, do not be tempted to make them serve on committees or expect them to take on significant additional responsibilities. If they are interested and willing, then seek ways for them to become more involved in departmental processes, but avoid piling on additional requirements.

Chapter 6 Summary and Questions

In this chapter we...

- **Reviewed best practices for hiring new faculty.** Doing your due diligence in attracting and hiring quality faculty will reap rewards for your department for many years, or even decades, to come. This means that you should start all hiring steps as early as possible, advertise widely, build a stellar hiring committee, and be well prepared for interviews and salary/benefit negotiations. Also, be prepared for a lengthy process with bumps in the road. Rarely do things work out very simply and neatly for the institutions that are hiring or the candidates themselves.

- **Discussed how to best support early career faculty.** Faculty who have just acquired their PhDs or emerged from post-doctoral programs will benefit immensely from your mentorship. They may be sharp as a tack with ambition to boot, but the wisdom and guidance you can offer early career faculty will help them hone their efforts and manage their expectations.

- **Considered the unique aspects of working with associate professors, adjunct faculty, and lecturers.** Each category of faculty will have particular issues and concerns that are relevant to them alone. Associate professors are considered mid-career professionals who ought to be well on their way to success in research and teaching, but keep an eye out for those who may have developed some ambivalence about their careers or who are dealing with issues that affect their job performance. Adjunct faculty and lecturers fulfill a critical role in shoring up a department's teaching gaps, so be sure to consistently monitor and meet their needs.

Answer the following questions to learn more about how the chapter content applies to you personally.

1. What general qualities make a faculty member a "good hire" for a department? How can you determine (with as much certainty as possible) during the hiring process if a faculty candidate possesses these qualities? On the flip side, what "red flag" qualities should you look for during the hiring process?

2. Reflect back on your first few years as a newly minted university faculty member. What advice, opportunities, and mentorship were offered to you then that significantly affected your decisions, priorities, and career trajectory? How might you offer the same (or better) to young faculty in your department?

3. Consider the adjunct faculty and lecturers in your department. In what ways are they regularly supported and mentored? Do they feel truly included in the department and participate in department-level initiatives? Can you think of any ways to assess and aim to improve the experiences of adjunct faculty and lecturers in your department?

Chapter 7.

Mastering Department Chair Duties

MASTERING THE DUTIES of a department chair is a process that requires time, diligence, and careful planning. You should thoroughly understand your role and responsibilities as department chair, and, as I have said many times before, you should be well aware of the departmental processes that are already in place and the policies that guide them. Now more than ever, department chairs should aspire to be strong leaders with great communication skills and empathy for those around them. Creating a vision, developing a strategic plan, leading by example, and motivating others with authenticity are some of the ways that you can truly "master" the role of department chair.

While it may seem that all your duties and goals are disparate and too numerous, you can make things more manageable by prioritizing and setting goals as a function of time. Four to five years is ample time to settle into the department chair role, observe what could be improved, and develop strategies to implement cohesively. After all, one of your primary goals should be to leave the department in a greater place than you found it. In this chapter, I will discuss several "nuts and bolts" issues that come up for every department chair, such as how to handle problems among faculty, how to assess faculty performance, and how to manage committees. Don't expect that you will handle every situation and every aspect of being a department chair flawlessly. If you're taking the time to read this book, you're clearly someone who is invested in becoming a successful chair! But you should challenge yourself to grow and improve each year in all aspects of your job. Eventually, with enough practice and determination, you may one day feel that you have "mastered" many of the duties associated with your leadership role.

Dealing with faculty (and staff) problems

If you inherit a department or are currently leading a department where the faculty get along well, do their jobs, and allow you to do your job as department chair, then consider yourself very fortunate. Better yet send me an email—I'd like to spend some time in your department to see how that works! Jokes aside, there is no such thing as a perfect department with no personnel problems. Faculty may voice complaints to you directly for any number of reasons, and it is nearly impossible to know what's coming around the corner. The best piece of advice I can provide is this: stay calm, and navigate every complaint carefully.

Complaints can take on many forms and be delivered in different ways. An unhappy or disgruntled faculty member can either walk into your office and voice a complaint or use a more formal approach and set up a time to discuss an issue with you. Recognize that not all faculty members approach a problem the same way. Some may be data-driven and highly professional, explaining the problem with an even tone of voice. Other faculty members can be volatile and emotionally distressed when discussing problems.

Many times, complaints can be handled amicably at the department level assuming that the department chair and faculty can communicate in a reasonable, clear manner. However, if issues are not easily resolved, they may quickly escalate to the next level, and the faculty member may file an "official grievance" that now brings other administrators into the fray. Depending on your university, this could mean that the dean, provost, or someone in the HR department becomes involved. If the faculty member files a grievance citing issues with diversity, equity, or inclusivity, you probably have another office on campus that handles that as well. If the faculty member feels that the university did not address the problem according to his liking, then they may take further steps to seek external counsel with an attorney. Taking this action will necessarily involve your university's office of legal counsel and will ensure that the issue takes a very long time to resolve.

So, what could these complaints be about? Just about anything! Issues regarding course assignments, travel funds, office space, funds for GRAs, committee assignments—the list goes one. Before I specifically discuss how to handle these confrontations, I want to be clear that I do not assume that the chair is always correct or that the faculty member is always correct. Both faculty members and department chairs can have unreasonable opinions, make inflammatory statements, or simply be outright wrong. Here are some guidelines for pursuing conflict resolution.

- If a faculty member walks into your office and begins to share a complaint, it is best to listen—for a short period of time—then ask the faculty member to set a time to discuss the issue in more detail. Also,

Handling faculty complaints and issues is a typical part of a department chair's duties.

ask the faculty member to send you a short summary of the complaint so you can review it before you meet. Remember that not all issues require such a formal approach, though. Sometimes it could be a simple misunderstanding or miscommunication, and as quickly as the problem started, it can go away with a bit of clear communication. Employ a more formal approach for bigger issues that will clearly require more than a quick conversation.

- Documenting issues that emerge is going to be key, especially if you have multiple meetings with the same faculty member. Ask your AA to be present for these meetings to take notes so that everything is recorded for you to review later or pass along to another administrator, if necessary. Also, if your AA takes notes, you will be able to focus more on practicing effective listening (see Chapter 5).

- If you feel like the complaints or issues being raised are related to guidelines in the department or university's process manuals, be sure to have them handy during the discussion. They can often provide immediate clarity and help you explain and justify your position on policies and decisions.

- Needless to say, you must always be professional—even if the faculty member becomes visibly upset. It really helps to maintain an even tone of voice. If you find yourself feeling emotionally triggered, try some quiet deep breathing or sip on some water or coffee while you listen to the faculty member share his or her perspective. Also, try to remember that the faculty member likely is not directly upset with you (although that could be the case). More likely, they are upset about a set of circumstances, and you are simply the person that they feel may have some power to address them.

- There's no reason to be intimidated by faculty, either. You should never feel coerced by someone who is acting aggressively.

- Sometimes a faculty member can become truly volatile. You need to take control of these situations by politely getting up from your chair and asking the faculty member to leave. Tell them that you can meet with them again after the situation has deescalated. At this point you should strongly consider contacting someone at the HR office to become involved or at least be aware of what has occurred. If a faculty member ever physically threatens you, do not hesitate to ask your AA to call the campus police or do so yourself. They will be able to help manage the situation and escort someone out of your office, if necessary.

- After you complete the meeting with the faculty member, send a short email describing what you discussed and a list of any action items (and to whom they are assigned). This should assure the faculty member that you are taking the issue by being responsive and action oriented. Always foster a fair, equitable, and transparent solution process.

Diversity, equity, and inclusion (DEI) infractions are common types of contentious situations that could involve anyone in your department, even you. For the past decade or so, most universities have trended in the direction of more seriously addressing accusations of harassment, racism, cultural insensitivity, sexism, etc. Investigating allegations of this nature requires significant time and sensitivity, and the outcomes may create long-lasting effects. If your university has a DEI office, it's always a good idea to include them in communications when these types of situations arise, and often HR will need to be involved as well. Below I've described a few of many possible scenarios that can arise when working to resolve DEI issues within your department.

- If a faculty member files an official DEI complaint and the university determines that a violation did occur, then typically all faculty members involved in the situation will be required to go through additional DEI training. Depending on the severity of the incident, some faculty members could be reprimanded further. The consequences may be quite significant if you, as department chair, are accused and determined to be in violation of DEI standards. If you are found "guilty", you could be required to relinquish your department chair title and be reassigned to the professor level. Regardless of whether this happens or not, rifts among the faculty will arise because not all faculty members will agree with the university's decision.
- If a complaint lodged by a faculty member is deemed to be inconsequential or untrue, usually no major outcomes will emerge from the

situation. The faculty member may believe that the university did not do due diligence, and they may continue to seethe about the situation. This can affect their work and professional relationships. Also, in my experience, the same faculty member is likely to file another complaint down the road. Universities often treat such issues with "kid gloves." As one department chair put it, "*Universities often do not have the guts to put a complaining faculty member on notice, meaning that they promise to take stringent actions if another complaint occurs and is found to be baseless.*"

Ultimately, a faculty member who constantly complains about DEI-related issues tends to become isolated, and other faculty would rather not deal with them because they are apprehensive of this repeated pattern of behavior. Many faculty will think "*I could be next!*", so they tend to distance themselves from potential trouble. In some cases, with a lot of work, it may be possible to bring this faculty member into the fold of the department by having numerous conversations, getting the FM to be more involved, and providing mentorship and mediation to resolve issues before they happen. While I am not a pessimist… this rarely works out well. The department simply has to resolve itself to the fact that the disgruntled faculty member will likely always have an ax to grind about something. In this case, as department chair, you will have to take the brunt of this!

Let me end this section by saying that I hope you do not have to deal with extremely contentious situations. Most faculty and chairs are willing to work together to solve problems, working out comprises that satisfy as many perspectives as possible. However, it is quite possible that you may encounter a faculty member who will persist in escalating situations. In that event, document all meetings and communications, and keep your dean and HR informed. Most chairs that I talk to say that only a very small fraction of their faculty cause the most problems, and that may be the case for you as well. However, recognize that sometimes these types of confrontations are inevitable. Be civil, courteous, and extremely professional in your approach. Let off steam when you're far away from campus, if needed.

Assessing faculty performance

I have yet to meet an administrator that absolutely enjoys evaluating faculty performance each year. While this is only one portion of your duties as a department chair, it is often a difficult process to objectively evaluate each faculty member. There are numerous books and research papers written about various evaluation strategies, but it is always difficult to design relevant metrics and scoring systems for teaching, service, and research that are tailored to your department.

Some people think there is one ideal, infallible method of evaluating faculty performance... but you aren't one of them, right? I certainly hope not. I'm warning you now that this will be one of the most difficult aspects of your job: seeking a fair, equitable, and objective approach to qualify and quantify your faculty's job performance. At some universities you may not have much latitude to select an evaluation method. You may be confined to a generic, university-wide rubric. If you have the opportunity to select your own, though, be sure to consult many resources on faculty evaluation and consider forming a committee within your department to gather input from your faculty. Even with this inclusive approach, be prepared that you cannot and will not satisfy everyone, and evaluation results can quickly lead to conflicts.

Several challenges must be addressed to create a functional and fair evaluation process. It is critical for the whole department to have a clear understanding of how faculty are rated. The first thing to do is determine the rating categories or ranks. Typically, the ratings include Excellent, Very Good, Good, Satisfactory, or Unsatisfactory, but there are numerous similar versions. It is common to associate every rating with a numeric value. Excellent could be 5, Very Good could be 4, Good could be 3, etc. And of course, to complicate matters, there could be a Very Good + worth 4.5, Good + as 3.5, and so on. Why are these ratings and numbers necessary? Each year on campuses throughout the country, merit pay raise information is assembled for faculty. As part of this process, your dean will require an evaluation of each faculty member and an overall rating so she can assign dollar values to ratings. Therefore, for faculty members, a lot is riding on how this rating system is structured and applied. Let's get into some more details about how faculty performance relates to these rating systems.

First, it is important to know if relative weighting is assigned to teaching, research, and service. For example, in a certain department, research may be weighted more strongly than teaching, or vice versa. It is very rare that service is weighted significantly for faculty. Let's say that the rating structure in a particular department is research = 50%, teaching = 40%, and service = 10%. Clearly defined guidelines should be codified for what constitutes excellent to poor performance in each category. Are faculty assessed based on the number of peer-reviewed publications submitted or accepted in that calendar year? the number of active grants for that year with a certain dollar value? the number of conference presentations? the number of graduate students supported by grants and contracts? Each of these potential metrics and many more must be considered, and documents should be drafted (and approved by upper administration) that articulate how faculty are assessed in each category. Be sure to also take into account that faculty will be in different stages of their careers, so perhaps there should be alternative assessment systems based on career length.

Arguably, it is even more difficult to measure teaching efficacy. Should it depend on the number of courses taught and the number of students in each of those courses? How should student evaluations of an instructor (SEIs) be weighted? As I have listened to faculty discuss SEI scores, whether they receive high ratings with good comments or poor ratings with scathing comments, they all seem to agree that the SEIs are not particularly informative or robust measurement tools. Often the number of SEIs submitted is low despite attempts by the administration to encourage professors to administer and collect them. Students who do well in a course typically do not participate in the process. They feel they have no helpful insights to offer about how to improve the course and are usually satisfied overall with the quality of instruction they received. So, a few disgruntled students who receive poor grades end up comprising the majority of respondents, submitting negative rankings and scathing reviews. Despite the downsides of SEIs, most universities continue to use them in faculty assessment.

As department chair, one major thing to realize is that a one-size-fits-all approach often does not work when assessing faculty performance. Unfortunately, you may not have much choice if upper-level administrators wish

Always be open with your faculty about how their job performance will be assessed.

to standardize evaluation metrics across multiple departments or within a whole college. If you do have latitude to design and alter evaluation practices, start with a careful review of current evaluation processes, and suggest mild to moderate changes each year. Too much change all at once can leave faculty feeling unsure about what is expected of them.

Faculty assessment needs to be an open and transparent process so faculty fully understand how they are being evaluated and scored. As department chair, you need to be able to explain all aspects of this process and be prepared to defend your position. The system that you use must be equitable and fair; people's livelihoods depend on it. It is also important that your yearly faculty performance assessment matches the merit pay raise (if one is available) that year. When it comes time to submit assessments to determine merit pay raises, department chairs may be tempted to "flatten the ratings" to provide the same (or just about the same) pay raise for all faculty members. This is not a good practice because it will upset the high performers and deflate their morale.

Managing committees

Some issues cannot be resolved by the faculty at large and require more concentrated work. Therefore, department committees can provide an avenue for some of this work. You may inherit a department that already has several departmental committees in place. For example, there may be department committees that evaluate graduate applications, assess curriculum, review qualifying exams for PhD students, and much more. It is your responsibility as incoming chair to first assess if these committees are actively working to accomplish their goals. Sometimes committees are formed simply because it feels like the right thing to do, but these committees hardly ever meet in person and work with focused effort. If a committee is really necessary, then by all means go ahead and keep it, but make sure there is a clear mandate and concrete goals.

Once I heard a faculty member say, "*My department chair avoids doing work by simply assigning work to committees.*" If faculty feel that you are dumping work on them that you should do yourself, then resentment will build, and committee members will feel like they are being asked to take on unnecessary "busy work." It's not wrong or unfair that you want them to do "extra" work for the sake of the department, but they may feel that whatever they have been tasked with should be on your plate, not theirs. You are at an impasse.

I always ask department chairs to automatically assume that their faculty are busy conducting research, teaching classes, and managing other duties, and the job of a chair is to alleviate administrative burden on faculty. I am not saying that you should never involve faculty, but if you ask a committee to write a first draft of your department's strategic plan—good luck with that! Truly, it will never be completed. It is a good approach to roll up your sleeves and do the "heaving lifting" on major departmental planning and activities and then seek input from faculty at the appropriate time.

Carving out time to do all the things that you are asked to do is challenging for all members of an academic department.

When all faculty are working well together, committees tend to run smoothly as well. However, there is often one faculty member who wants desperately to serve on a particular committee, but you may feel he or she is not the not the appropriate fit for that sort of committee. Before you get blamed for not being inclusive, you need to make sure that all your committees have bylaws, term limits, and a process by which members are elected to the committee. This is much easier done when committees are initially formed, but if you come to the department as a new chair and find that there is no standard process established to elect committee members, it's up to you to advocate for such a process. This will save everyone a lot of frustration.

Here are some practical strategies for forming and managing committees:

- First, obtain a list of department committees including committee members and committee leads. Committee leads, or committee chairs, usually report back to the department chair about the committee's ongoing progress.
- Find out the term limits of committee members and how members and leads have traditionally been elected/selected.
- Post department committees on your department website and also on a communal display board so everyone is aware of the roles and responsibilities.
- Dissolve committees if there is no clear purpose for them and if they have not met for a long period of time.
- Form new, relevant committees if needed depending upon the needs and vision of the department.
- Empower committees to make appropriate decisions, and encourage the committee chair to make presentations at faculty meetings to keep other faculty informed.

A paragraph, page, or an essay?

Well, you were going to find out sooner or later—this job will require writing, writing, and more writing. As department chair, you will quickly learn that you will often be asked to write memos, letters, documents, strategic plans, and justifications that could consume a lot of time. And even when you think you've fulfilled your obligations, the dean or someone else will ask you for more information or further clarification on top of what you have already provided. Knowing how much to write and at what "depth" is always tricky. Some documents require elaborate research and a lot of critical thought, while other documents merely serve as place holders in a larger document and will not need much refinement. Documents like a negative reappointment letter may require multiple pages and carefully crafted sentences. Alternatively, your dean may ask for your opinion on a matter and only be looking for a short paragraph. Here is what one dean had to say about communicating with department chairs. *"I wish my department chairs would pay more attention to what I say at meetings. On one hand, they complain that I ask for too much information and need it in short order, and on the other hand, when I ask them explicitly for just one paragraph or a few bullet items, they send long documents full of unnecessary information."* While it is admirable that these chairs want to do due diligence in all their written documents, it is wise to learn what to write and how much to write when asked for input. Writing too much can lead to frustration for a chair as well, because if their feedback is not thoroughly reviewed, they will feel that their time was wasted, and their opinions did not matter.

Department chairs should be in the habit of referencing requirements in official documents. For example, if criteria for tenure is listed in a process manual in a short paragraph, then simply reference the paragraph when needed. You can quote sentences and sections directly to ensure that you did not miss any of the requirements. Here is an example of a letter recommending an associate professor's promotion to full professor:

As department chair, I provide this recommendation based on section 7.1 of the faculty handbook that states, *"A professor must have the terminal degree in a pertinent discipline, except where the individual has achieved equivalent status through outstanding performance. A professor also must have attained authoritative knowledge and reputation in a recognized field of research or creative achievements and must have maintained high levels of effectiveness in teaching and in service."*

Dr. Sampras is an accomplished scholar with authoritative knowledge and a strong reputation in the field of land-atmosphere interactions. He has published more than 50 peer-reviewed papers in reputable journals with an impressive citation index (Google Scholar: 9757 citations, h-index 41, i10-index 50). He has also contributed to seven book chapters and 50 conference papers... (and so on).

The department process manual

A thorough and readable department process manual can help tremendously with avoiding problems, inefficiencies, and conflicts. If you are a department chair who was fortunate enough to inherit a mature, smoothly operating department with a strong process manual—consider yourself lucky. However, there is always room for improvement. This is especially true if there are mundane processes that have not been automated. Even in departments that have been in existence for multiple decades, it is quite possible that a department manual (or process manual) may be nonexistent or poorly constructed. As department chair, it is important for you to realize that a strong manual is your ally. In many situations you will be able to point your faculty and students to the manual for guidance or reference the manual yourself when you are trying to make a big decision.

Here's what one faculty member had to say, *"I was really interested in serving on a certain department committee. I really felt that I could add value. So, I approached the department chair via email and in person and expressed an interest in serving. However, the chair was not very responsive. She seemed to want to keep the same committee composition, and after some digging, I found out that the members of this committee had remained unchanged for many years. Surprisingly, they hardly ever met to resolve issues or provide recommendations. I felt left out, confused, and disappointed."* This is exactly where you do not want to end up as a department chair. This situation caused the faculty member to feel excluded and rejected. As department chair, you might think—who would create such a fuss about not serving on a committee? Most faculty in my department are extremely happy not to be asked or required to serve on committees. For most faculty that may be the case, but all it takes is one faculty member to raise an issue like this, and then you have to spend weeks and months sorting out the mess.

In the previous example, consulting a process manual could have been very helpful. Ideally, the manual would state how many committee members should serve on the committee, how they are elected, the term limits for these members, and the mandate or mission of the committee. If the manual contains all this information, then you could simply direct your questioning faculty member to the relevant section and encourage them to follow the outlined process to be considered for committee membership in the future. If the manual is lacking in details regarding this committee, then you can take the opportunity to draft new guidelines yourself and present them at the next faculty meeting for review and voting.

It is important to note that there is probably a process manual at the college and/or university levels, and you should refer your faculty and students to those manuals as needed. However, the manuals designed for the college or university should not be used exclusively at the department level. A separate process manual designed specifically to address department-level matters is absolutely necessary. Of course, it is good practice to vote on

What do I do if no department process manual exists?

Well... I think you probably already know the answer to this question -- time to get to work! Even though policies and manuals should already exist at the broader university level, you 100% need a manual that is tailored to the specific and unique aspects of your department. I don't recommend reinventing the wheel, though. Tap into your spheres of influence at your university and beyond. See if you can gain access to manuals used by other departments so you can formulate ideas about what should be included in your department's manual.

these process manuals at faculty meetings and record the discussions and votes. Be sure to provide a link on the department website to a digital version of the manual so that everyone can readily access it when needed.

Not that you would ever do this, but let's imagine what could happen if you don't take my advice on this topic. Have you ever had a department chair who never seems to be clear about processes? He often approaches tasks out of sequence, sends paperwork to the wrong offices and individuals on campus, and fills out forms incorrectly—all of which negatively affects faculty members and students. This is what I call sloppy management. One administrative assistant commented about her boss with this type of behavior, "*The department chair never seems to get a handle on processes. He keeps sending me things to do that actually require his attention, not mine. I can fill out necessary forms on his behalf, but I cannot write a recruitment plan!*" A faculty member in a similar predicament said, "*My department chair never seems to know how to advise me on certain affairs. I asked him how detailed my application for sabbatical should be, and he said write whatever, no one cares. Thankfully I talked it over with another faculty member who provided his sabbatical plan which was very detailed with required objectives and outcomes.*"

While these two situations may seem a bit extreme to you, I assure you these are two real cases. The department chairs either delegated work when it was not appropriate (signaling to the AA that he was lazy or uninformed) or dispensed terrible advice. In either case, the department chairs did perform due diligence by reading the university's process manual and following through in the correct ways. As department chair, it is your responsibility to do the following:

- Remove administrative burdens from your faculty, and don't make them search university websites and manuals for information that you should be providing readily.
- Do not lead faculty and students astray by giving them incorrect information. If you are unsure about something, do the work to find trustworthy answers and follow up with the pertinent individuals. If the information you find may be useful to others, consider sending an email to the whole department.

- For items that come up repeatedly, put together a Frequently Asked Questions section on your department's website and provide the appropriate links to download documents and forms. These could include how to request vacation time, how to write sabbatical applications, or how to write and submit a program of study for a graduate student. Scenarios like these come up often in the lifecycle of a department. Rather than delegating or providing wrong information, your department members will thank you for collecting reliable information and presenting it in an easily accessible format. It also benefits you by reducing the time required to answer these types of questions.
- Much like how undergraduate advisers have easy-to-use spreadsheets for every major on campus, develop a simple one for your graduate students. Making it available to students will answer many of their potential questions and allow them to take their program of study seriously, and more importantly, take ownership of their degree pathway.

Strategic Planning

Forward-thinking departments usually have a strategic plan in place that can be easily accessed by all stakeholders. The plan is usually displayed prominently on the department's website, and it provides a broad roadmap for a range of years specified in the document. Stakeholders are not only faculty, staff, and students within the department, but also others who have a vested interest in the department's success.

Strategic planning exercises can take many months or even years to complete, depending on the size of the organization and the complexity of the intended goals. Typically, university-level strategic planning will involve external consultants and a team of internal and external stakeholders working together to identify priorities and draft the roadmap. Often one of the first things that university presidents do is to initiate a strategic planning process because it demonstrates their initiative and vision. (And frequently these strategic planning exercises come with a hefty bonus for the university president... for better or worse.) While the scope of the departmental strategic planning is quite different than what occurs at the university or college levels, it is important to make sure that your department-level strategic plan dovetails with the big picture view. As chair, it is ultimately your responsibility to ensure that your strategic plan makes sense from all angles; otherwise, your plan will be insufficient.

There are numerous steps on how to initiate and complete a strategic plan and entire books have been devoted to it. In this section I will provide some key elements of a strategic plan and how to engage various stakeholders to create a roadmap for the future.

1. **Gather stakeholder input.** Without stakeholder input, the strategic plan will only reflect your personal interests and views. No matter how good your intentions, it's wiser to aim for a thorough, collective plan developed from many stakeholders. Input from faculty members is of paramount importance. You should communicate with all faculty

about the details of the process, being clear that you are spearheading the strategic planning exercise and that its success relies on their feedback. A good opportunity to share these ideas is in a faculty meeting, and you can follow up by providing a timeline for plan development.

In some departments, forming a committee is the first step of crafting a strategic plan. If you have faculty who are willing to actively participate on a committee or in this venture in general, then you are bound to have success. Often faculty have very little time to devote to helping write and edit a plan, but they may be willing to offer input occasionally throughout the process. Very few faculty members are going to roll up their sleeves and volunteer to assist with the entire document. I strongly suggest that you gather input both formally and informally in one-on-one and group meetings. Use your notes from these meetings to begin outlining the document in broad strokes based on the concerns, perspectives, and ideas that you gather. Seeking input from staff and students is also critical. Depending on the size of your department, you should also consider engaging with other stakeholders (e.g., donors) to gain their perspective. Discussions, surveys, and focus groups are all tools you should consider using.

2. **Conduct a self-study analysis.** Consider yourself lucky if your former chair left you with a detailed self study of the department complete with strengths, weaknesses, opportunities, and threats (SWOT). A self-study analysis usually provides important information on the history of the department and key metrics such as enrollment, retention, graduation rates, awards won, and a whole host of other information. Examining a self study will allow you to identify major department trends over the past several years. These types of statistics are usually available at the institutional level, and if your predecessor did not put together a self study, you can task your staff assistant to obtain the information to assemble one yourself. These statistics will be the foundation to not only gauge the pulse of the department but to justify requests for resources.

   Moreover, keeping track of these data along with outcomes will go a long way towards developing documents for the accreditation process. If an accreditation process exists in your university, maintaining these documents on a continual basis is much better than waiting to draft them until they are requested. Once a self study is complete, set a schedule to revisit it every year or two to update the document. Also consider inviting external evaluators (e.g., another department chair) to review the self study and offer insight into how your department is functioning relative to others.

3. **Draft a mission and a vision statement.** In theory, a mission and vision statement for your department may seem easy to write, but it is downright difficult to get the wording fine-turned so that the statement is meaningful, truthful, and not too overreaching. They are supposed to be inspirational, but don't inflate the language so much that the statement becomes "fake." A vision statement usually looks to the future while the mission talks about what the department is currently doing. Remember that it is a good idea to incorporate your department's core values into these statements. The sentences should be clear and concise—not multiple paragraphs with numerous bullet points. If you are fortunate, you may have a senior member of the department who absolutely enjoys this type of thing. You can rely on him or her to wordsmith every tiny detail of these statements to produce a polished product.

4. **Articulate goals, objectives, action plans, and performance indicators.** This is the bulk of the strategic plan. Developing these aspects of the plan is probably the hardest part of the process because it requires numerous discussions, a 360-degree evaluation of all stakeholder input, and a careful assessment of strengths and weaknesses. Typically, it is best to define three to five goals for the department and to articulate objectives, action items, and performance indicators for each goal. Goals could include topics like strengthening certain thematic areas, driving digital innovation, or increasing faculty, staff, and student diversity. Do not hesitate to glean from the wisdom of other department chairs in your university who have done this before. Your dean should also be able to provide guidance and pointers.

Also remember that numerous departments around the country have gone through a similar exercise, so you can ask to review their strategic plans and gather ideas about document tone and structure. In my experience, department chairs and colleges who have gone through this process are eager to share not only the documents they produced but also advice about potential pitfalls. Therefore, it may be wise to communicate with as many department chairs as possible. However, at the end of the day, you have to "own" your department's strategic plan. As department chair, you need to be able to provide a succinct overview of the strategic plan when asked.

Below is an example of a goal with objectives, action items, and performance indicators.

Goal: Increasing Faculty and Student Diversity

Begin with an opening paragraph that provides some introduction and rationale to this goal. It should articulate reasons why prioritizing inclusivity and diversity is important for students, faculty, and staff. Also include some statistics about current levels of diversity and how this goal will improve outcomes.

- **Objective 1: Recruit a diverse and inclusive workforce.** (Usually, there are two to four objectives for each goal.)

  - **Action item 1: Collaborate with and create pathways for historically underrepresented students to enter the department.**
    Provide details on how the objective will be achieved—typically four to five action items for each objective. The action items must be realistic, achievable, pragmatic, and aligned with the goals of the college and the university.

- **Performance Indicator 1: Number of students entering the department from historically underrepresented universities**
  State a metric for each action item to determine to what degree the goal is being achieved.

1. **Determine resource allocation.** If you thought coming up with the goals, objectives, action plans, and performance indicators was hard, then take a deep breath. Resource allocation is up next. All the grandiose goals of wanting to be a top ten department, hiring new faculty, empowering students to go to conferences, hiring a diverse workforce, creating a state-of-the-art laboratory and much more require money, and lots of it.

   As department chair, you must be careful when navigating the world of budgets and fundraising. Likely, you will want to know upfront from your dean what resources are available for a strategic plan. However, you may get a "standard answer" of "*Well, come up with a plan, and let's see what it looks like.*" That's usually a bad place to start because you may not know all the details about the budget landscape of the university, and the dean is in a better position to know such things. Administrators often want to see an increase in enrollment, retention, and other measures (the bottom line of the university) before agreeing to investing funds into your department.

   This is the classic "what comes first problem." Funding a department requires a plan, but it's difficult to create a viable plan without knowing what and how much you will have to work with. Let me also say this—if your department, college and university have a history of going through expensive strategic planning exercises, but inadequate or no resources were provided to fund any plans that emerged, then you and your department shouldn't bank on ever receiving a windfall from the administration. Therefore, be cautious about encouraging faculty to put in a lot of time and energy into the strategic planning process if you have a sense that you will not reap many benefits in the end. Wasting time is a sure way to discourage faculty from engaging in future department-wide planning efforts.

2. **Evaluate progress.** A well-designed strategic plan should be held accountable. This means that progress should be monitored, measured, and evaluated regularly. Depending on the size of the department and the resources available, this could be done by a team of people, or as chair, you may find yourself doing the bulk of the work. You may have to do this periodically (once every semester), and you should seek ways to involve faculty and staff, if possible. If your department has a "retreat" at an off-campus location, this could be a great opportunity to set aside time to evaluate outcomes of the strategic plan. Keep in mind that not all plans should be immutable. Strategic plans that are very rigid often have limited success because they are written for a three-to-five-year period. In evaluating your department's progress so far, you may realize that some adjustments are needed for action plans or performance indicators.

3. **Maximize partnerships.** Developing and maintaining partnerships is vital to the lifeblood of any academic department. Being siloed in the world of academia shortchanges both faculty and students. Therefore, developing a spirit of collaboration should be a key part of any department.

   There are numerous avenues for fostering collaboration and partnerships. The most typical method involves partnering with organizations and donors to increase funding for the department. These types of partnerships certainly boost the department's resources and profile. In return, it looks good for local companies and organizations to support your department's research and students. For example, a public health department could work with an engineering department to address pollution issues. Not only does a project like this provide hands-on experience to engineering students, but it also addresses needs in the local community.

   Another way to develop partnerships is by building on-campus relationships. There are excellent opportunities for interdepartmental collaboration through cross-listing courses to provide internship and research opportunities. However, building successful plans and programs with another department can require significant time and perseverance. For instance, a biology department could reach out to a computer science department to discuss how to design a course in computational biology.

Think of partnerships as several layers of influence. The first level is within your college and university, and it could include departments, research centers, and other offices on campus that can help launch you into partnerships. The next level is outward facing where, depending on your department's academic discipline, you could develop partnerships with relevant industries. Some universities have the luxury of being collocated with research parks, and these companies are always looking for innovative solutions that your faculty and staff can provide. The final level is what you choose to make of it. Partnerships can reach beyond your regional and state boundaries, extending to national and international arenas. There are no limits, really—only creativity and a willingness to collaborate is required.

4. **Enhance educational and research programs.** This is likely one of the major reasons you took the job in the first place—to enhance educational and research opportunities for your faculty and staff. So, this should be the fun part of the job! If you have a forward-thinking department that has been developing self studies and both short-term and long-term strategic plans, then consider yourself lucky. Some departments do this extremely well, assessing department culture, resources, goals, and plans often and adjusting as necessary to stay on track. Other departments struggle to adhere to a regular cadence of departmental evaluation and maintenance. Regardless of how "well oiled" your departmental machine may be, you can always identify opportunities to develop both the educational and research aspects of your organization.

As department chair, you are probably in the best place to learn from and interact with other chairs across the country and globe. You also have the opportunity to attend workshops and seminars that are specifically geared towards department chairs.

Your faculty are hard at work doing their jobs, and they have very little time to think about how departments are evolving under the influence of new ideas, trends, and business models. Therefore, it's up to you to take the lead in identifying and exploring concepts that could enhance the department's functionality.

An assessment of the strengths and weaknesses of your department should clearly tell you if the department has stagnated in certain areas. For instance, consider the role of machine learning (often referred to as "artificial intelligence") in education and research. If your department has buried its head in the sand and not addressed ways in which students could benefit from machine learning in the curriculum, then you are doing students a disservice. Machine learning is a prime example of a technological approach that is already affecting practically all fields of research. If your department is ignoring its influence, then the curriculum you teach will quickly become stagnant and outdated.

Chairs need to always remain focused on what they can do to best serve their students and faculty. Therefore, bringing new ideas to your department is your responsibility! The same goes for hiring new faculty. Some departments are merely "one deep" in certain thematic areas, with a single professor filling a niche role. Enhancing the education enterprise into new areas that will benefit your department and the university is critical. As department chair, you may have the opportunity to develop specialized course offerings, new degree tracks, or entirely new programs— the possibilities are numerous. I have even known department chairs who have worked diligently to establish entire PhD programs where none existed before.

Another approach to enhancing the educational and research programs in your department may require investing in new facilities and resources. While expensive, it may be necessary to keep your department moving in a positive direction. You might need additional space, new furniture, or advanced laboratory equipment, and if your university is capable, then even multimillion dollar new buildings are possible!

5. **Foster diversity and inclusion.** Diversity, equity, and inclusion (DEI) measures should not be relegated to just one office on campus. Hopefully, the leadership throughout your organization—from the president down to the department chairs—are championing DEI on a regular and consistent basis. You, as department chair, have an excellent opportunity to educate and communicate these measures to your faculty. There are numerous strategies and actions that are possible from clearly communicating your commitment to DEI. You can articulate statements and policies tailored to your department, and you also have a unique vantage point to advocate for hiring practices that are fair and unbiased. Numerous campuses have DEI training available for faculty and staff. Depending on the size of your department, you could designate a "point person" to champion various DEI initiatives, such as mentorship and support programs for underrepresented students and faculty and affinity groups. You can also ensure that seminar speakers and other guests that you invite to your department are diverse, which will broaden the perspectives of your entire department.

6. **Communicate the strategic plan.** As chair, you have put in all the hard work to get to this point, but the plan cannot come to life without clearly communicating it to everyone it will affect. Sharing the strategic plan with stakeholders is absolutely critical. There is no one-size-fits-all approach when it comes to communicating the plan and the processes involved. Mature departments often make their entire strategic plans available on their web site. However, they also know that not all stakeholders are interested in the entire plan or have the time to digest it all. Therefore, developing shortened plan summaries (and maybe even an infographic) is a helpful way to easily communicate the "nuts and bolts" of the plan. Yes, this means more work for you, but it's truly a necessary part of the process if want the plan to be supported and implemented successfully.

    Strategic plan presentations to the dean and provost and others in your university should be detailed with various data, strengths, and weaknesses. Also include a description of how your plan fits into the university's high-level strategic plans. You may also present the strategic plan to other departmental stakeholders such as donors or industry sponsors. Be sure to carefully consider the interests of each audience, and modify your presentations as needed to be engaging and informative for different groups.

7. **Review and update the plan.** Even when it is complete, a strategic plan is what I would call a "living document." As chair, you will not only shepherd the process of its development, but also you must continue to be its caretaker as it is put into action. Therefore, periodic reviews should be planned as part of the plan's implementation and maintenance. As I mentioned before, there may be emerging trends in workforce requirements or in research areas that you may need to consider in light of the strategic plan. It may feel frustrating at times to never be truly "done" evaluating and modifying a strategic plan, but remember that, like so many things in life, a good plan needs some flexibility and adaptability to be as successful as possible.

8. **Celebrate achievements.** A "finished" strategic plan document is definitely a cause for celebration and probably a vacation earned for you as department chair! However, it is your responsibility to keep your team focused on the central goals and how they are achieved. Therefore, celebrating every milestone is important for the morale of your faculty. Celebration events for faculty and sometimes with stakeholders will go a long way towards building the reputation of the department. Find appropriate ways to advertise the success of the departments in various venues to ensure that the department's achievements are acknowledged beyond your organization.

Chapter 7 Summary and Questions

In this chapter we...

- **Considered how to handle complaints and issues involving faculty and staff.** Dealing with grievances is often one of the most difficult parts of serving as department chair. No matter what kind of complaint is delivered to you, the most important actions you can take are to listen carefully and document everything. Resist the urge to try and "fix" everything immediately. You need to gather facts and probably talk to other individuals who may be involved before attempting to resolve a situation. Also be aware of when a dispute is at a level that you can manage and when you ought to call in other administrators or departments (like DEI and HR) for assistance.

- **Discussed methods of evaluating faculty performance.** Most faculty in your department are likely quite good at their jobs and try in earnest to meet high expectations. However, no faculty member is perfect, and just like in corporate jobs, periodic assessments can be both informative and motivating. If you are given some freedom to decide how to evaluate faculty performance, then you should review a wide variety of assessment rubrics and solicit faculty input on what would work best in your department. If you must instead use a standard college- or university-wide assessment tool, then do your best to communicate with your faculty about how they will be assessed and be as objective and thoughtful as possible in reviewing their performance.

- **Highlighted best practices for forming and managing committees.** A small, focused group of faculty can work wonders by digging deeply into an issue or brainstorming creative solutions. They are a necessary component of a smoothly functioning and forward-thinking department. Avoid going overboard in creating committees and conscripting faculty members to serve on them, though. Try to reserve committee work for issues or initiatives that are particularly inspiring to your faculty members and make sure that you do not task them with "busy work" that could be accomplished by you or someone in your staff.

- **Emphasized the importance of a department process manual and a strategic plan.** Reading a manual is probably nobody's idea of a good time, but having a detailed, clear department process manual available to everyone in your department can resolve an awful lot of questions and tricky situations. If you are deeply familiar with the manual to the point that you can easily direct your faculty members and staff to certain sections when needed, then others will catch on to the importance of this document as well. An equally important document is a tailor-made strategic plan for your department. Creating a strategic plan that is both ambitious and achievable is no easy task, but having a roadmap to guide your department is a critical step towards enhancing your organization's educational and research opportunities.

Answer the following questions to learn more about how the chapter content applies to you personally.

1. Think back to an instance in which you (as a student or faculty member) voiced a complaint or aired a grievance to a professor or administrator. If you can't recall ever doing this, then ask a colleague to share one of their experiences. How did the authority figure respond to the situation? Do you think his or her response was appropriate and effective? Was the resolution fair and sensi-

ble? If you had been in the authority position, how would you have handled the situation differently?

2. Imagine that a disagreement between two faculty members in a faculty meeting turns heated. It becomes clear to everyone present that the faculty members harbor resentment that has developed into an interpersonal conflict. As chair, how would you address the situation in the moment? How would you plan to follow up with the faculty members?

3. If you were fully in charge of designing a faculty assessment rubric (and maybe you already are!), what would it look like? What categories would you assess, and how would you count each category (by percentage) in an overall evaluation? How would you go about assessing faculty—would you observe a class that they teach? Gather feedback from their graduate students? Count their citations in peer-reviewed journals? Try to strike a balance between thoroughness, fairness, and feasibility.

4. If you are in an academic department in any capacity, try making a list of all committees currently operating in your department. Is there an easy way for everyone in the department to access a committee list and some information about the purposes of the committees and the work they have accomplished so far? If this information is difficult to find, how might it be shared more broadly with your entire department?

Chapter 8.

Planning Your Next Move

WHETHER YOU PLAN TO move up the administrative chain in your university or leave to pursue another administrative opportunity (or decide to head back to your own department to resume your activities as a professor), formulating an exit strategy is a must. In this section, we will discuss how to carefully prepare for a smooth transition to the next phase of your career.

Face it, after one or two terms of being a department chair, you will probably be ready to move on to your next challenge. It may seem like a myriad of options are available, but it is never easy to make a decision. When you stepped into the position of department chair, you probably hadn't thought much at all about where you might go next in your career. Even while you pour 100% effort into your department chair role, it is wise to give some attention to what your next move will be and how you will manage it. Looking forward to the next phase of your life should be done with a sense of purpose. If I make it sound easy, it is not! I had to go through this myself a few times, and while I may have agonized over the options, I always ended up prepared for my next career phase.

Keep in mind that this decision-making process will often involve more than just your personal interests and wishes. Planning major next steps in your life usually includes soliciting the input of family members, friends, and others, because you are part of a broader community. Let's take a closer look at the most likely options that you might entertain after your tenure as department chair.

- **Option 1: I'm ready for Round 2!** As you near the end of your designated time as chair, perhaps you decide that you want to continue as department chair for 4- or 5-year another term. Just because you want to continue in this role does not mean that you will automatically be granted the opportunity, though. There is usually a reappointment process at universities in which the dean has to solicit comments from faculty and others and then formally decide if you can continue in the position or not. Usually, you will know even before this process occurs if you will be reappointed or not. If over the last 4 years you had mishandled situations and there were a lot of faculty and student complaints about your leadership style, then you should probably not expect to be granted reappointment.

  There may be various compelling reasons for you to seek another term as chair. Remember that usually your pay is higher because as chair. You will typically receive a paycheck for all 12 months of the year (as opposed to 9), and you may also receive a stipend. Another reason could be that you still have some unfinished business. Perhaps you started a strategic plan and you have successfully completed 50% of those initiatives, but you are eager to tackle the other half. You might wish to stay on for a few more years to see these efforts through to completion. Whatever your reasons may be, it is important to let your dean know that you wish to continue as chair. She may offer some thoughts about whether or not she supports this idea. Do not take it too personally if the dean is in favor of hiring a new chair, though. She will have to consider many competing pressures to determine what may be the best next step for your department. Fighting this decision will only lead to more acrimony, because even if you were to be reappointed, you will have to work with the dean fully knowing that her first choice was to replace you. That is not a great position to be in because she is someone who you will want on your side when it's time to advocate for your department. Give your dean a gracious exit strategy, and it will do everyone a world of good.

- **Option 2: Climb the leadership ladder.** As you were serving as department chair, you probably thought at least once about what it would be like to transition to a different leadership role at your university. That's great, because universities need good department chairs who are willing to consider stepping up to the next level. As the Aussies say—good on you! As chair, you will have a great vantage point to see how the college is run from a ground-up perspective. Your regular interactions with the dean and your interactions with other department chairs will provide you with wisdom and insights.

  Sometimes it is possible that you will have the opportunity to apply for the dean's position at your current university if the dean is planning to retire or move into a new position himself. One thing to note is that, in most cases, dean positions are nationally competitive, and as an internal candidate, you may not be given any special consideration. The selection process is lengthy and could take up an entire year. This means that while you are serving as department chair, you will be writing a resumé, participating in interviews, and going through the same set of hurdles as all other candidates.

  There are advantages and disadvantages to being an internal candidate. As department chair, you will be very familiar with the strengths and weaknesses of your college, from personnel to research funding to budgetary issues. If you have been at the university for a while, you will likely already have several spheres of influence, as well. This means that you know who to contact if there are problems that need to be addressed, and you hopefully have built a good rapport with many contacts. On the other hand, it is quite possible that the university will be interested in hiring an external dean with more established credentials and experience. The applicant pool may very well include candidates who have already served many years as deans elsewhere. Also, even if you had a relatively successful run as department chair, other chairs in your college may not be keen on reporting to you if you became dean.

  Nevertheless, there are always bound to be advantages and disadvantages for external candidates as well. Applying to be a dean at another university with no prior experience in the role can be a bit of a long shot. Besides not knowing the university very well, you will also not be intimately familiar with how to function as a dean. Ultimately, this may not be a concern for some universities, though, if they determine that your credentials, vision, and personality are a good fit with their school.

- **Option 3: Return to professorship.** Some department chairs serve one or two terms and feel that they have had their fill of academic administration. They are ready to head back to the department to teach, do research, and serve the department in other capacities. If you find yourself feeling this way, it is important to let the dean know as soon as possible so she has ample time to conduct a search for the next chair. Leaving the chair position and going back to the department may seem easy because, after all, you have plenty of experience in that role! This is why, if you ever have any intention of returning

Returning to professorship may be the right choice for you after finishing a cycle as department chair.

to the department, it is important to continue teaching at least one course per semester or per year. It is also important to stay involved as much as possible with research. Teaching and doing research while fulfilling all the duties of a department chair may seem like a tall order, but it sets an example for your faculty and paves the way for an easier transition back to the department.

- **Option 4: Retire.** Depending on the stage of your career, maybe you will feel ready to finish out your time as department chair. Some universities may even offer you an Emeritus Chair title—quite the honor! While this could be seen as the culminating moment of your professional career, you need to make this decision carefully. You simply can't be too prepared for retirement.

  While there are numerous books written about retirement that discuss finances, what you will do in retirement and how this will affect your family members is rarely mentioned. It's up to you to think through this deliberately and make a plan. One of my colleagues retired in June, was thoroughly bored by the time October came around, and decided to start part time work in November at two days per week. In less than a year, he was back to full time doing the same types of things he was doing before retirement. Another colleague put together a 3-day a week, 18-hole golf schedule and built his entire retirement around it. He once told me, *"I served as dean for nearly 10 years, and it is high time I made up for all the golf time that I've missed."* He traveled to golfing events and also vacationed across the world. He was content and made the most of his post-working years. Another colleague immersed himself in volunteer work after retirement. He worked with various private donors to raise funds for children who did not have the ability to pay for lunches in middle and high schools.

  Numerous options exist, and as a good friend of mine who retired mentioned, *"I thought that I was going to have so much fun getting up as late as I wanted every day. I also thought that I could spend a lot of time at the beach and in the mountains. But after several months of this, I was truly bored. I quickly realized that, even in retirement, I needed a schedule—something to look forward to and to give me purpose. I rec-*

ognized that my health and mind would suffer if I did not refocus and find a solution." This is why it is in your best interest to always be considering your next steps and making plans for every phase of life.

Retirement or a reduced work schedule is enticing to many former department chairs.

Final thoughts

I hope that I've adequately conveyed how essential a good department chair is to create a smoothly functioning academic department. With effective, consistent leadership, you can propel the department to higher heights. You can provide the necessary support to motivate faculty, empower staff, and engage the student body. A department that is on the same page will likely be a department that excels at all levels. Achieving this goal is no easy task. It requires dedication, perseverance, and plain hard work. Of course, you will encounter many challenges and rewards along the way.

Achieving your goals as department chair can feel like climbing to the summit of a mountain.

Always keep in mind that you are the keeper of the culture of the department. If you are diligent and disciplined in your work, then your colleagues and staff will likely notice and follow your lead. If you shirk your responsibilities or put in minimal effort, then a negative slide is bound to ensue. Your leadership style can have a powerful impact on those around you, so choose your words and actions wisely.

While the journey to becoming chair and then stepping into the role is exciting, be aware that your day-to-day experiences may be fraught with speed bumps. This is because you are leading *people*, and each person will harbor his or her own opinions, desires, and perspectives. You can avoid many issues by learning how to navigate situations even before they happen, which is hopefully something that this book has taught you. Finally, remember that no job is worth sacrificing your personal life, including your physical, mental, and emotional health.

Best wishes as you contemplate and explore leadership opportunities. Enjoy the ride!

Chapter 8 Summary and Questions

In this chapter we…

- **Considered possible next steps you could take after serving your term as department chair.** As the end of your term as department chair approaches, you may be confident in your next move, or a bit ambivalent. If you had a positive experience as chair, then you may wish to continue in the role for another few years—maybe you have some unfinished business to resolve or a clear vision for a new initiative that you are sure will benefit the department. You may also be interested in exploring new administrative opportunities at your university or beyond. Alternatively, you could resume your position as a full professor in the department or even opt to retire. Any of these options can be the right choice, depending on your personal goals and interests.

- **Reflected on what it means to be a good leader.** A truly invested, diligent department chair can change the culture and course of an academic department dramatically. Rallying the troops, while drafting a vision plan, while responding to never-ending emails, while planning faculty meetings, while managing a budget… well, you will never really feel "done" for the day. But a good leader knows how to put 100% effort into everything they do and maintain boundaries to keep themselves healthy and balanced.

Answer the following questions to learn more about how the chapter content applies to you personally.

1. You may not have a definitive answer to this question yet, but are you interested in pursuing other academic leadership positions beyond being a department chair? If so, what are some action steps you could take to better inform yourself about the responsibilities of the positions you are interested in?

2. It's never too early to start thinking about retirement, or at least your goals for retirement! What is on your retirement "bucket list"? What do you hope to accomplish as a department chair and in your professional career overall before you move on to the next chapter of your life?

Acknowledgments

I am sincerely grateful to the many individuals who have provided unwavering support and encouragement throughout the process of writing and completing this book.

My heartfelt appreciation goes out to Rachel Wyatt, whose dedication to editing and coordinating various crucial aspects of this book has been instrumental in shaping its final form. Her keen eye for detail and commitment to excellence have been invaluable.

I extend my special thanks to Shaelyn Lozier and Allison Jowers for their incredible talent in creating the illustrations.

I am deeply indebted to Lori Wheeler for her unfaltering support, ensuring that my professional responsibilities remained intact and manageable during the arduous journey of penning this manuscript.

Lastly, I want to express my profound gratitude to my beloved wife, Sheba, and my three wonderful children, Grace, Samuel, and Abigail. Their enduring love, patience, and belief in me have been my constant motivation to strive for excellence in all aspects of life.

To all those whose names may not be mentioned but have played a part, big or small, in this endeavor, I am truly thankful for your contributions.

Thank you all for being a part of this journey and for making this book a reality.

About the Author

Dr. Sundar Christopher is a professor and King-McDonald Eminent Scholars Chair in the Department of Atmospheric and Earth Science at the University of Alabama in Huntsville. He has served in various leadership positions including Department Chair, Dean of the College of Science, Associate Director of the Earth System Science Center, and Director of the Institute of Remote Sensing Applications. His research interests include satellite remote sensing of clouds and aerosols and using satellite data to study the impact on air quality, health, regional climate, and the environment. Dr. Christopher has served as Principal Investigator on numerous grants and contracts, been selected to several satellite science teams, and has published more than 125 peer-reviewed papers in national and international journals.

Dr. Christopher particularly enjoys teaching and mentoring students and faculty. His first book, *Navigating Graduate School and Beyond*, is widely used to counsel graduate students and their advisors. His second book, *Navigating Tenure and Beyond: A Guide for Early Career Faculty*, assists faculty in establishing and following successful career paths.

Appendix A.

Case Studies

Case studies are just that—case studies. While you may think that the case studies shared here are from my personal experience, this is not actually the case (pun intended). I field questions very regularly from department chairs around the country and in my own university about "hypothetical situations." You may or may not be able to relate to the couple of case studies presented here, but rest assured you will encounter similar situations some day!

Case Study 1:
Assigning equitable course loads

If you have a group of faculty members who very easily comply with your teaching requests and assignments, then I want your job! Jokes aside, teaching assignments can become sources of conflict for a variety of reasons. While the university wants maximum productivity from a faculty member in all aspects of their work, it is simply not possible to find even a single faculty member who can do everything at the 100% level. Maximum productivity to a university for a faculty member may look like this:

- On the research side: Write and win as many grants and contracts as possible, attract many quality graduate students, and write a lot of peer-reviewed papers that garner many citations.
- On the academic side: Teach several classes without teaching assistants, use office hours and one-on-one tutoring to support students, and lead curriculum development.
- On the service side: Serve on departmental and university-wide committees, attend recruitment events, and support university initiatives.

For most faculty, fulfilling all of these expectations all the time is simply unreasonable and unattainable. For instance, you may have several high-quality faculty who are heavily involved in funded research, so it is difficult to expect them to teach a heavy course load at the same time.

Most universities have faculty course load guidelines per semester and per academic year. Colleges usually follow those guidelines or may sometimes adhere to slightly different standards depending on the makeup of the departments with the college. For example, it is not out of the ordinary for the "College of Arts" at a university to require their faculty to teach 3-4 courses per semester. In the same university, faculty within the College of Engineering may only be required to teach two courses per semester because of research expectations.

Now comes the tricky part. It is also highly probable that if there are multiple departments in a college—let's say, the College of Science that may house departments such as biology, mathematics, physics, and computer science—there are many potential disparities to reconcile. The number of students enrolled in certain classes and the number of grants/contracts for each faculty member may differ significantly. Some courses may have additional lab components, while others may not. What if one of your faculty members feels strongly that they are being treated unfairly with the number of courses they have been assigned to teach? Let's explore this situation with a case study.

Associate Professor Sonia in your department has about 1.5M in funded grants and contracts with five students that she supports with her research grants. She is also actively pursuing further collaborations and opportunities for research. Associate Professor Mark, who has been in the department for a while and is considered a senior member, has no research grants and contracts and writes very few proposals. In theory, based on their research workloads, it is not equitable for Sonia and Mark to be required to teach the same number of courses to the same number of students. However, this is where things get messy. Maybe your department already has some solid policies outlining what constitutes a course load, but following those guidelines will result in unbalanced responsibilities for Sonia and Mark. If you feel strongly that the guidelines should not be followed precisely for the overall good of the department, you should take this dilemma to the dean and propose your solution. Speak individually with Sonia and Mark about what they feel is fair, and share your thoughts about what you feel are reasonable course loads for each of them. Then, make it a priority to follow up on re-evaluating the course load policy structure and presenting a revised version at a faculty meeting.

A fair, consistent, and explainable course load framework is the responsibility of the department chair. If a department chair cannot explain course assignments clearly to the faculty and to her dean, then trouble is right around the corner. With a fair system in place, the faculty will usually be agreeable. However, the minute they get wind that they are teaching more courses or students while maintaining a heavier research load compared to another faculty member, they will be knocking on your door sooner rather than later.

If you encounter a contentious faculty member who is not happy about her course load, then it is your responsibility to have a clear-cut discussion on how you arrived at your decisions. Making too many exceptions to the rule book will invariably erode your credibility and leadership status.

If your course assignments are fair and objective and driven by clear policies, then any faculty members with an issue should understand that the course assignments are final with little opportunity for negotiation. However, course assignments should not be made in a vacuum. Before courses are posted on the university website, you should ensure that all faculty and administrators have had the opportunity to engage in discussions and voice any concerns. Explain to your faculty why your decisions are important for the collective good of the faculty. Faculty look out for one another, but they rely on fairness and competence from the department chair in navigating these situations.

Case Study 2:
An early career professor who wants to date a graduate student

If you think that this situation rarely occurs in universities, then you are sorely mistaken. The dating pool for young professionals often includes people who they interact with at work or in their classes. Most universities do not have clear policies concerning these circumstances, and complicated issues (that must be handled delicately) may arise without proper guidance. Keep in mind that some universities do have certain policies about relationships between professors and students, and if that is the case, it is your job as department chair to follow the guidelines and ask questions as needed. So, how might you handle things if a graduate student and professor come to your office to announce their relationship and ask for your advice? Or if you simply hear about the budding relationship "through the grapevine"? Here is how one department chair I know dealt with this type of situation.

In the words of the department chair, this is how it all began.

"It was a seemingly normal week, and I saw on my calendar that one of my faculty members wanted to see me regarding a personal matter. Glancing through my calendar, I noticed another appointment with a senior female student, and the calendar again indicated that the meeting was about a personal matter. At that time, I did not connect the dots. In my usual fashion, I stepped into the conference a few minutes before the first appointment and waited for my faculty member. He seemed unusually nervous and uncomfortable upon his arrival. After a few awkward minutes filled with small talk and hesitations, he finally said that he wanted to embark on a romantic relationship with a female student, and he mentioned the name of the student. Now I began to "get it." I listened, took notes, and told him to give me a few days to check university policies

and send him any information that I found. Walking back to my office I shook my head and thought—well, that was not in my job description! The meeting with the female graduate student was very similar, and I told her that I would also provide her with more feedback soon. I thanked both of them for notifying me about the emerging situation."

The department chair contacted his dean, and the dean strongly encouraged him to check in with the university attorney in the office of legal counsel. He continued his story:

"The university attorney was a seasoned individual, and he made me feel very welcome to his office. He asked me to start by sharing what was discussed in the meetings with my faculty member and the graduate student. He took notes, asked a few questions, and then he leaned back to offer counsel. He said 'Look, these things happen, and there is no way you can forbid anything. Be glad that they came to you seeking advice. Now, you need to take care to manage this properly and document any official meetings carefully so there are no loose ends.' He offered advice on setting 'firewalls' between the faculty member and the student in the department. He wisely recommended that the student not be allowed to take courses taught by the faculty member or be allowed to serve on any committees under his leadership. Finally, he told me to outline the details of the "firewall" in writing and submit the document to him for review."

The chair dutifully constructed a document that listed allowable and unallowable actions between the graduate student and professor. The document stated clearly that the student could not take courses taught by the faculty member, the faculty member could not serve on this student's advisory committee, and the faculty member could not be present when discussing students in faculty meetings. He indicated that the hardest thing to figure out was how to "socialize" the relationship between the faculty member and the student. The attorney indicated that they should take the lead themselves in allowing other department members to know about their relationship. If questioned, they could share that the chair had established protocols for how they could interact professionally.

The chair then met with the faculty member and the student together and explained how the department and the university had agreed to proceed with firewalls. Thankfully, both had no objections and thanked the chair, dean, and attorney for their guidance.

While you may never encounter such a situation, it is entirely possible. Love often blooms close to home! The key to handling this situation is to establish thoughtful protocols and processes and keep a close eye on the situation to make sure that the guidelines are being followed. It is wise to periodically update the dean and the office of legal counsel as well.

Appendix B.

Department Chair Survey Responses

I sent an informal survey to several current or former department chairs. Most of them were currently serving as department chairs, and some had just finished their stint in this academic position. Here is the one question that I posed to each of them:

What are the top three things that you wish you had read in a book or someone had told you about being a department chair?

Below are some of the responses that I received.

- I would have liked to have known better how to work with faculty to develop a vision and a feasible strategic plan to elevate the department to the next stage, how to manage time effectively for multiple tasks as a department chair, and how to facilitate effective communication between the faculty and the college leadership team.
- Easy. Faculty are not your friends. They're lazy and totally self-absorbed, with no sense of the good of the department. Students will always blame someone/something else for their failings or problems and expect the chair to fix it. The most important thing is to just care. And this will lead to endless aggravation and disappointment, but you know you've done your job.

- Don't assume that faculty think about things (finances, teaching, etc.) the same as you; they often have very different motivations and priorities. For example, whereas I am always thinking of how the group will be funded, I have some faculty that essentially never consider finances in decision making (most often to their detriment). Interpersonal relationships among the faculty, as opposed to other considerations like their research, etc., often impact their decision making when it comes to things like nominations and voting. This one might be the most obvious, but 90% of your time will be spent on problems as opposed to department building. Worse yet, the problems always come up on short notice and addressing them can't wait—regardless of what else might be going on!

- 80% of your time will be spent on dealing with issues raised by 20% of your people (faculty, staff, students, etc.). Even though all faculty are highly educated, some can be as illogical or unreasonable as anyone you could encounter. Mentality or psychology can be very powerful and consistent in forming one's behavior.

- I am always looking for insights into emotional intelligence. Understanding people is the most important task as a chair—especially when balancing the needs of students, faculty, and staff. I would have liked to know more about the ability to persuade others of the importance of organizational needs at the sacrifice of their own, because everything else pales in comparison. Personal management, "calendaring" key tasks, and clear note taking for the next person to occupy the seat are also things I would have liked to have been more prepared to handle.

- There is one thing I wish I had been told in advance—deans are busy people and can easily forget verbal commitments they make. Be sure to document everything in writing.

- I would have liked to read some tips on getting people to open up and tell me what they really think, which I have found to be a real issue with junior faculty. They are afraid of me even though I have told them repeatedly that I am on their side regarding career development, promotion, etc. I also would have liked more preparation in how to interact with my dean to get what my department needs without sounding selfish. This is an important issue since we just had a new dean. It was also difficult to know how to restructure my research team to maintain productivity; my research is taking a hit right now. I am learning to better manage my time, but I realize that I need a middle manager kind of person to take care of some routine tasks while I am being pulled into department administration.

- The only unexpected thing so far is that the dean scheduled the school leadership meetings to coincide with our departmental seminar slot. Hoping to get that changed!

- Give situations time. So many issues solve themselves or de-escalate with a little patience. In fact, I would say that patience is the best skill to develop. Also, open the books. Let people know the scale of the department's resources and how they are divided. Be willing to break with tradition if needed if it is unfair. Pick a few goals to improve the department over time. Stick to them, and nudge the department forward when the opportunity arises. Presidents, deans, faculty, etc. all come and go, but you can be consistent, especially when pursuing the greater good.

- I wish I had been told to seek training. Seminars, workshops, and/or conferences specifically for department chairs are very much needed. I didn't fully understand my role or how to manage it. There was no HR-led orientation, no current chairs, or other administrators to guide me. Trial and error and learning on the job were challenging and time consuming. It always seemed like I was behind, playing catch-up. People were not forthcoming with basic information. I relied heavily on my administrative assistant's network (until she accepted another position). After two years of searching for workshops (during Covid), I participated in a 2-day seminar specifically for department chairs. It included virtual sessions and round table discussions of current issues and concerns. It was great to connect with and learn from other department chairs and division heads. We were all overworked and underprepared. We had a brief opportunity where we shared best practices. Several of those suggestions, I was able to employ immediately. But this only touched the surface. There is a need for weekly or monthly sessions on different topics from the department chair perspective (e.g., budgets, hiring, promotion/tenure, time management, conflict resolution, FERPA, self-care, etc.). I also wish I had known more about how to get connected. Try to communicate and build relationships with other department chairs. Join the Chairs Council (if one exists on campus) to discuss issues, best practices, hiring, general faculty/student concerns, etc. with them. Also, connect with classmates or colleagues already in your network who are chairs or division heads. Finally, getting a mentor is key. I needed someone who could be a sounding board, share wisdom, experiences, and strategies, ask hard questions, provide a safe space to vent and cry, and offer encouragement. It's important to always be authentic. Stay true to your values, faith, and character. Make an effort to understand your budget and change it to support your department goals.

- The number of students who need overrides (special permissions to enroll in courses) and the number of reasons for the overrides is daunting. I also learned that faculty have little motivation after tenure to participate in campus recruiting and student development activities. Also, although you specifically tell junior faculty what is required of them in reappointment letters, they don't read the letters closely and follow the directions.

- In my case, I was extremely experienced with department administration before finally getting the title. However, I was surprised by local deviations from the norm that are unique to my university. For example, all positions are a half step down here. That is, the chair is an "associate chair plus." The dean is a "chair plus." A connected phenomenon is the volume of staff work I'm expected to do myself. I'm expected to be my own media department; I operate all the cheating appeals (used to be a DoS staff function), etc. That comes from running way too lean here—not a nationally ubiquitous problem. I tell my staff that I'm the best admin they will ever have. The other local crazy-making issue is the annual reappointment cycle for tenure-earning faculty. I think most realize this is actually damaging, but no one will fix it. Again, something that is unique to my university. So, I guess the answer to your question is that someone should have told me how localized the interpretation of the job can be. The chair's job at my university is not the same job at other places. Put another way, the chair at a #100 school won't be the same job as at a state flagship school. Resources largely control the experience.

- Some of the things I wish I had known more about include: managing a departmental budget; resolving conflicts (especially between faculty and students); dealing with faculty (and students) who are disruptive and lack discipline; dealing with unprepared and dishonest staff members; managing the workflow; and coping with faculty who are resistant to changes that have been suggested by either the chair, the dean, or the administration.

- It would have been great to know better how to deal with differences in opinions and how to build consensus among the faculty. This includes how to tackle or reconcile the vision difference between the college leadership and your own faculty unit. Also, I wish I had known to ask for more clarity from college leadership regarding resources I would have access to as chair.

- Stepping into the job of department chair generally comes with very little administrative training. I wish someone would have let me know the importance of serving as an advocate for myself, especially in connection with asking many questions when stepping into the position. This includes sometimes posing questions to those who have the information we need—and who think we should already know it—yet there's no logical reason that we would already know it! I wish someone would have told me that effective department chairs can possess many different personalities and leadership styles, but that one common factor that can be highly effective, regardless of personality or leadership style, is to reflect a sincere level of care and respect for colleagues/staff/students at all levels. I wish someone would have told me to seek out training connected to computer/online administrative processes, such as Native Banner, that may be totally unfamiliar to us in our position as regular/non-chair faculty. Students often encounter technical barriers that keep them from enrolling (such as permissions to enroll for a course), and being extremely familiar and comfortable with the computer processes that can fix any problems such as this that students encounter can go a long way in students feeling supported by their departmental administration. In connection with this, I would add that the registrar's office can be a huge help, and it is worthwhile to get to know the registrar and their staff. I wish someone would have told me, prior to stepping in the position as chair, to learn as much from the current chair (shadowing if necessary) as possible, since there are so many tasks that experienced chairs take for granted that they do daily, and they may be totally unfamiliar to an incoming chair. (This gets back to serving as an advocate for oneself—in this case, prior to stepping into a chair position.) Finally, I wish someone would have told me that the best way to "shine" is to serve as a mentor, and in some cases, a cheerleader to allow others (often younger, less experienced colleagues) to "shine." The successes of those who report to us can have a much greater impact on others' perception of us as effective leaders, rather than spending most of our time advertising our own greatness.

Appendix C.

Additional Resources

While I have high hopes that this book will be exceptionally informative and motivational specifically for department chairs or those aspiring to become chair, I would be remiss to not mention other available books and resources about academic leadership. Please use the non-exhaustive collection below to add more suggestions to your personal reading list. Remember, you cannot read too much about how to be as successful as possible in your career!

Buller, J. L. (2011). *Academic Leadership Day by Day: Small Steps that Lead to Great Success.* San Francisco, CA: Jossey-Bass.

Buller, J. L. (2012). *The Essential Department Chair: A Comprehensive Desk Reference (Second Edition).* San Francisco, CA: Jossey-Bass.

Chu, D. (2006). *The Department Chair Primer: Leading and Managing Academic Departments.*

Chun, E. & Evans, A. (2015). *The Department Chair as Transformative Diversity Leader: Building Inclusive Learning Environments in Higher Education.* Routledge.

Creswell, J. W., et al. (1990) *The Academic Chairperson's Handbook.*

Gmelch, W. H., & Miskin, V. D. (2004). *Chairing an Academic Department.* Madison, Wisconsin: Atwood Publishing.

Gmelch, W. H., & Schuh, J. S. (2004). *The Life Cycle of a Department Chair.* San Francisco: Jossey-Bass.

Hansen, C. K. (2011). *Time Management for Department Chairs.* San Francisco, CA: Jossey-Bass.

Hendrickson, R. M., Lane, J. E., & Harris, J. T. (2012). *Academic Leadership and Governance of Higher Education: A Guide for Trustees, Leaders, and Aspiring Leaders of Two- and Four-Year Institutions.* Stylus Publishing.

Higgerson, M. L. (1996). *Communication Skills for Department Chairs.* San Francisco, CA: Jossey-Bass.

Leaming, D. R. (2007). *Academic Leadership: A Practical Guide for Chairing the Department.* Bolton, MA: Anker Publishing Co.

Lucas, A. F., & Associates (2000). *Leading Academic Change: Essential Roles for Department Chairs.* San Francisco, CA: Jossey-Bass.

Maxwell, J. C. (2001). *The 17 Indisputable Laws of Teamwork.* Nashville, TN: Thomas Nelson Publishbers.

Sternberg, R. J. (2015). *Academic Leadership in Higher Education: From the Top Down and Bottom Up.* Rowman & Littlefield Publishers.

Wheeler, D. W. (2008). *The Academic Chair's Handbook.* San Francisco, CA: Jossey-Bass.

Index